Ferrari

333 SP

Other great books from Veloce –

www.veloce.co.uk

For post publication news, updates and amendments relating to this book please visit www.veloce.co.uk/books/V4758

Cover photographs: Front cover: The Baldi/Velez 333 SP undergoes a routine pit stop at Watkins Glen, in 1995. (Courtesy IMRRC Watkins Glen)
Back cover: 333 SP #011 in the paddock at Road Atlanta,1996. Theys and Jackson, driving, finished fourth. (Courtesy Martin Spetz)

First published in May 2015 by Veloce Publishing Limited, Veloce House, Parkway Farm Business Park, Middle Farm Way, Poundbury, Dorchester DT1 3AR, England. Fax 01305 268864/e-mail info@veloce.co.uk/web www.veloce.co.uk or www.velocebooks.com.
ISBN: 978-1-845847-58-6 UPC: 6-36847-04758-0

WSC GIANTS

Ferrari

333 SP

Terry O'Neil

VELOCE

Contents

Acknowledgements and data sources

Simply to say "thank you" to the people who have helped with this book is easy. However, to truly express my gratitude to those same people who have given of their most valuable commodity, their time, which is priceless, is nigh beyond me. Suffice it to say that I am extremely appreciative of the help that they have given.

In no particular order they are: the staff of the International Motor Racing Research Centre at Watkins Glen, the Ferrari Owners Club, Dean Butler and the National Motor Museum at Beaulieu.

Also to those people who have provided me with wonderful photos for the book: Keith Bluemel, Peter Collins, Peter Grootswagers, Andrew Hartwell, Gary Horsikorta, Paul Kooyman, Gerry McDermott, Martin Spetz, Tom Schultz, and Helmut Schnug.

Reference has been made to the following publications:

Autocar & Motor
Autosport
Autoweek
Cavallino
Ferrari Owners Club magazine
Motoring News
Prancing Horse
Time and Two Seats

Terry O'Neil

Introduction

The ever-increasing claims on Ferrari of money and manpower to sustain the technological demands of Formula One racing saw the demise of its sports prototype production for endurance racing in 1973.

Some 20 years later, Ferrari was persuaded to re-enter the realms of sports prototype racing. This unexpected, but very welcome, addition to the line-up of sports prototype racing cars for the 1994 season came as a surprise to many people in the sport. The Prancing Horse from Maranello was to take its place on the start grid of the IMSA World Sports Car Championship races after a 20-year absence from the track, not, however, as a factory-entered team, but rather in the hands of several privateers. While the privateers bought the cars from Ferrari, the factory and Ferrari North America provided all the necessary technical support for the privateers at each event.

The initiative for the project came from veteran racer and founder of Momo, Gianpiero Moretti. He saw an opportunity provided by the new US endurance IMSA rules for the Ferrari factory to enter cars on a competitive basis. It was not easy to convince the Ferrari factory to build the car, but Moretti gained vital assistance from Piero Ferrari, then manager of Ferrari's Special Projects Department, and support from Gian Luigi Buitoni, President of Ferrari North America.

Twenty years' absence from this extremely competitive area of motor racing was a very long time in anyone's book, especially when year-by-year on-going product development was the norm during the 1990s. Constant rule changes enforced on manufacturers did nothing to reduce the escalating costs of entering the events, as the World Sports Car Championship had taken 33 different forms

Gianpiero Moretti

Gianpiero Moretti, founder of the Momo Company, was born in Italy in 1940. He was the main instigator in persuading Ferrari to produce the 333 SP. He ran, and raced for, Momo, achieving his life-long ambition of driving as part of the winning team at the Daytona 24-hour race in 1998.

Gianpiero Moretti.
(Courtesy Andrew Hartwell)

since its inception in 1953. Assured that it would not affect the Formula One programme budget, the project, named 'Il sogno Americano', was authorised by Ferrari President, Luca di Montezemolo. The price of the car was announced at $900,000, but, for that, the car came with two spare engines, and a considerable amount of spare parts. Moretti committed to purchase the first car produced, and pledged that it would showcase Ferrari racing and technology in the USA.

Ferrari power-train engineer, Mauro Rioli, was in charge of the project, assisted by Tony Southgate; Giorgio Camaschella designed the body. The first car was built by Ferrari and refined, after extensive use of Dallara's wind tunnel, under the control of Dialma Zinelli. Testing commenced in mid to late-1993, followed by an initial production run of eight cars. The chassis of the first four cars were built by Ferrari; the remainder by Dallara. The first deliveries were made in February 1994 to three teams that would campaign the cars: Scuderia Momo (Gianpiero Moretti); Scandia Motorsports (Andy Evans); and Euromotorsport (Antonio Ferrari).

Within the competitive working lifespan of the Ferrari 333 SP, the cars were entered into five major Championship series. In America, they were: the IMSA World Sports Car Championship (later to become the Professional Sports Car Racing World Sports Car Championship); the United States Road Racing Championship Can-Am; the American Le Mans; and the Grand-Am Rolex Sports Car Series. In Europe, there was the International Sports Racing Series; as well as Le Mans.

The results for the car were remarkable: 47 victories scored in 126 races, including 12 Championships.

Last-minute checks on the Momo 333 SP #003 before practice at Mosport 1996. (Courtesy Andrew Hartwell)

Car specifications

1994

The Type designation '333' referred to the historic Ferrari method of naming a car after a single cylinder displacement, while SP signified 'sports prototype.'

Jointly developed in conjunction with Dallara, the Ferrari 333 SP was designed specifically to comply with the new IMSA WSC prototype regulations. IMSA regulations specified that the engine used could not displace over four litres, and had to be derived from a road car. The engine was derived from Project F130, more commonly known as the F50. The V-12 engine incorporated four camshafts, and five valves per cylinder, and was initially a Formula One engine, before being increased in capacity to 4.7 litres and de-tuned for the F50.

The engine was again partially de-tuned, and had the stroke shortened, so as to end up with an engine size of 3997cc, hence conforming to the IMSA limit of 4-litre capacity. The unit was fed by a Weber-Marelli digital fuel injection system, and was attached to the gearbox at one end, and at the other end to the carbon fibre/aluminium honeycomb tub, which itself had derived its origins from the Formula One tub.

The drive-train consisted of a sequential mechanical gearshift mechanism with five speeds plus reverse. The transverse gearbox was mounted within the wheelbase of the car and coupled to a limited slip differential.

The front end of the car was filled with radiators; the independent double wishbone suspension was bolted onto the sides of the tub at the front, and the gearbox differential casing at the rear. The old steel tube chassis was consigned to history; instead, a new carbon fibre composite was used. The body was constructed from Kevlar fibre/epoxy resin into large panels that could be easily removed to afford good accessibility to the working parts.

The wheels were 17in by 12in in front and 17in by 14in in the rear, and had Brembo axially-ventilated discs constructed of either steel or carbon fibre, depending on the rules.

Subsequent modifications

It was only natural that modifications were made to the 333 SP over time. They were not dramatic changes, more a case of evolution than revolution, with subtle differences appearing on the various team cars.

A new nosecone appeared from the factory in 1995, but it was generally accepted that this was mainly for aesthetic purposes; while among the teams, Scandia used a third shock absorber at the front as an anti-dive system, which appeared to work for it. A different windscreen was used on the 1995 cars, and repositioned side air intakes introduced.

In 1996, Momo developed closed flanks bodywork; a move that was studied and developed by Michelotto before Michelotto produced its 1998 version body. Also in 1996, the engine was given a major upgrade, and an alternative 'endurance' unit introduced which, although not increasing the performance noticeably, did increase its durability to withstand races such as Daytona and Le Mans. The modifications included a new head with smaller valves, and a different air filter.

The engine was further developed in 1997, when a new lubrication system in the combustion chambers and new pistons were introduced. 1998 saw the introduction of the new Michelotto closed flanks body from #017 onwards, with a strengthened chassis, and a six-speed gearbox. The new gearbox was legal for Le Mans and the European ISRS series; together with 18in wheels, which, in turn, allowed for larger brakes. Even as late as 1999, further development of the gearbox and front brakes on the endurance cars took place, and a different sprint specification engine was built with higher power output.

Ferrari had stopped developing its engine in 2000, so Kevin Doran (Doran Racing) replaced the ageing Ferrari V-12 engine with a Judd V-10 unit in chassis 025: far more competitive under the air-intake restrictor rules applicable in ALMS and Sports Racing World Cup regulations. The Judd was lighter, more powerful, had better fuel economy, and was cheaper than the Ferrari engine.

In Europe the GLV Brums team also went down the same route in 2001, but failed to improve the car's overall performance.

A chrome 333 SP badge affixed to the first few cars – but which quickly disappeared in the hands of souvenir hunters.
(Courtesy
Keith Bluemel)

The Ferrari 333 SP on display for all to see, prior to its first race outing at Road Atlanta.
(Courtesy Tom Schultz)

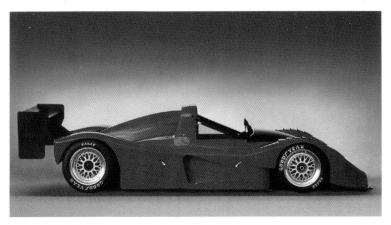

La Ferrari F 333 SP segna il ritorno della Marca nel settore delle vetture sport destinate ai clienti piloti. Nel rispetto della tradizione che ha accompagnato il successo sportivo e commerciale dai suoi primi anni di esistenza, approfittando della opportunità data dai regolamenti IMSA, la Ferrari propone questa barchetta biposto, prodotta in un numero limitato di esemplari. La vettura è venduta completa di un kit di carrozzeria, telaio e meccanica, in grado di garantire la gestione al massimo livello di efficacia nel corso della stagione sportiva.

Carrozzeria
L'efficienza e la stabilità aerodinamica sono il motivo tecnico di base per lo studio della carrozzeria. In fibra di carbonio e Nomex è caratterizzata da pannelli a aggancio rapido per l'accesso agli organi meccanici.

Autotelaio
Telaio portante in composito di fibra di carbonio e nido d'ape in alluminio. Sospensioni indipendenti a puntoni anteriore e posteriore. Guida destra. Freni Brembo.

Motopropulsore
Motore V 12 di 65°, 3997 cc. oltre 600 CV, posteriore, centrale, longitudinale. Cinque valvole in titanio per cilindro con distribuzione a quattro alberi a camme in testa. Iniezione elettronica digitale Weber Marelli. Lubrificazione a carter secco. Trasmissione con cambio trasversale, entro il passo, a cinque rapporti più retromarcia, a comando meccanico sequenziale. Differenziale autobloccante. Frizione a tre dischi metallici.

The Ferrari F 333 SP signals Ferrari's return to the production of sports cars for the gentleman driver. As a mark of respect for a tradition that dates back to its earliest successes in racing and in sales, Ferrari has taken the opportunity offered by the IMSA regulations to launch this two-seater produced in extremely limited numbers. The car is sold with a body, chassis and mechanicals spares kit that will keep it in tiptop shape throughout the season.

Bodywork
The body was designed for optimum efficiency and aerodynamic stability. Made of carbon fibre and Nomex it features panels that are quickly removed to give access to the mechanical parts.

Chassis
Stress-bearing chassis in carbon fibre composite and aluminium honeycomb. Independent pushrod-rocker suspension front and rear. Right hand drive. Brembo brakes.

Power train
65° V12, 243.2 cu.in., over 600 HP engine set amidships. Five titanium valves per cylinder with four overhead cams. Weber Marelli digital electronic injection. Dry sump lubrication. Transverse gearbox within the wheel base featuring five speeds plus reverse and sequential mechanical gearshift. Limited slip differential. Three sintered metal plate clutch.

Page one of the specification brochure given to prospective buyers of the new 333 SP. (Courtesy Keith Bluemel)

F 333 SP

Dimensioni e pesi		Dimensions and Weights	
Carreggiata anteriore	1,660 m	Front track	65.4 in
Carreggiata posteriore	1,572 m	Rear track	61.9 in
Passo	2,710 m	Wheelbase	107.9 in
Peso a vuoto	860 kg	Kerb weight	1896 lb
Serbatoio carburante	70 l (standard), 100 l (durata)	Fuel tank capacity	18.5 US gal. - 26.4 US gal. (endurance)
Cerchi anteriori	17"x10"	Front wheels	17"x10"
Cerchi posteriori	17"x13"	Rear wheels	17"x13"

Motore		Engine	
12 cilindri a V di 65°		12 cylinders in 65° V layout	
Cilindrata totale	3997 cc	Total displacement	243.2 cu.in
Potenza massima a 11000 giri/min.	oltre 600 CV	Maximum power @ 11000 rpm	over 600 HP

Page two of the specification brochure given to prospective buyers
of the new 333 SP. (Courtesy Keith Bluemel)

1994 – Vindication

The Ferrari 333 SP did not make the most auspicious of starts in 1994, as, prior to its racing debut, chassis 001 crashed with Mauro Baldi at the wheel, on one of the many test runs it was undertaking in an effort to iron out any faults and weaknesses. The heavy crash resulted in substantial damage, with #001 having to be rebuilt around a new tub, and it would not be ready to participate in the IMSA WSC race at Atlanta.

The first two rounds of the WSC series were held at Daytona and Sebring. Because they were endurance races in the true sense of the word, it was thought sensible not to enter the brand new Ferraris, as there were doubts about the durability of the titanium valves. However, Ferrari was shrewd enough to put a car on display at both venues to generate interest in anticipation of its race appearance. With its stunning looks, it was a car that simply commanded attention.

In the meantime, the team cars were meticulously prepared, and gently eased into the fray in the third round meeting of the IMSA WSC, held on April 17. At least two of the cars sported a feature that would soon disappear: a chrome 333 SP badge on the rear flank of the car.

Road Atlanta, Braselton, Georgia, April 17

Four new Ferrari 333 SPs turned up for the third round of the WSC series at the Road Atlanta 2.54-mile circuit, creating a stir among competitors and spectators alike. The Momo entry was driven by Gianpiero Moretti and Eliseo Salazar, while the Scandia Motorsports entry was in the hands of Ross Bentley and Andy Evans. The two entries from Euromotorsport were driven by Mauro Baldi and Jay Cochran.

Practice sessions produced some interesting results. The three quickest times of the day were made by Ferraris: Baldi was the fastest, followed by Cochran and Bentley/Evans. Fourth quickest was the Spice SE89-Chevrolet driven by Andy Rouse. During the race itself, any doubts about the seriousness of the Ferrari challenge were quickly dispelled. Baldi led the way for 50 laps, ahead of 14 other entries, before suspension failure put him out of the race on lap 65. This was the cue for Jay Cochran to take over as race leader. He drove faultlessly to victory, averaging a speed of 116.04mph, crossing the finish line over a minute ahead of the Moretti/Salazar Ferrari.

The marque had achieved a remarkable 1-2 finish on its return to sports prototype endurance racing. Asked for his reaction after the race, Cochran said to the *Hartford Courant* reporter, "It was the biggest moment of my career. I was patient. It was perfect. When I started the race, I had a plan and it all unfolded. I am confident about racing at Lime Rock. I feel confident about the car that, if it runs well, we will smoke everyone."

Lime Rock, Connecticut, May 30

Six weeks had elapsed since the previous race; a period in which the teams had time to reflect upon their fortunes at Road Atlanta. The teams fielding the Ferraris had more reasons to be pleased than most others; a theme that continued through practice as the high-pitch shriek of the V-12 Ferrari engine reverberated around the rolling hills of

Lime Rock Park. At the end of the session, the grid was set, with Salazar's 333 SP on pole followed by Mauro Baldi.

As the 15 entries sped away from the start, James Weaver's Spice DR3-Ferrari took an immediate lead, followed closely by the three 333 SPs of Salazar, Baldi and Cochran. The first pit stop shuffled the pack, with Baldi taking over second spot behind the Spice DR3-Ferrari.

The one hour mark proved to be a pivotal moment for Cochran; his 333 SP, #005, ran out out of fuel. Fortunately, the car had enough momentum to make it to the pits, but the episode cost him dearly. At the same time, the leading Spice-Ferrari retired due to brake problems, and Baldi's ill-fortune continued, with his car's suspension giving way again. The race was won by the Salazar/Moretti 333 SP #004, followed by Cochran, with Morgan/Evans in third.

The Moretti/Salazar car had led the race for 63 laps and averaged 101.24mph. It was bad luck for Cochran, as he was only 16 seconds behind the winning car at the end of the race.

Watkins Glen International Raceway, New York State, June 26

The race at Watkins Glen was to mark a new venture for the 333 SP. It had withstood the test of two-hour races; this race was three hours long.

Antonio Ferrari's Euromotorsport team had cut back on its efforts and leased one of its cars to Scandia Engineering, so only three of the 333 SPs turned up for Saturday's qualifying run. Salazar took pole position with co-driver Moretti. Behind him was Jeremy Dale's Spice HC94-Oldsmobile, Mauro Baldi in the second 333 SP, and James Weaver in Rob Dyson's Spice DR3-Ferrari. The final 333 SP, #003 of Evans and Cheever, was judged underweight and relegated to the back of the 44-car grid.

The start of Sunday's race saw Salazar sweep into the lead ahead of Dale and Weaver, a position he held until the first pit stop. Baldi never made it to the first pit, though, as his run of bad luck continued, when his 333 SP coasted to a stop, its engine expired and smoking, after 14 laps.

Consequently, co-driver Jay Cochran was denied his chance to shine.

With the second round of pit stops, Salazar was able to slip back into the lead, followed by Dale and Weaver. Towards the final laps of the race, electrical faults and a subsequent fire sidelined the Evans/Cheever 333 SP, leaving

Momo car #004, during practice at Watkins Glen.
(Courtesy IMRRC Watkins Glen)

The Salazar/Moretti 333 SP about to overtake Simone/Hoerr's Chevrolet Camaro at Watkins Glen.
(Courtesy IMRRC Watkins Glen)

The Scandia Motorsports car #003 was driven by Bentley and Evans to finish fifth at Road Atlanta. (Courtesy Martin Spetz)

Thorough preparation of the car was a key consideration for the Scandia team at Road Atlanta. (Courtesy Martin Spetz)

The Momo team car finished second at Road Atlanta, driven by Moretti and Salazar. (Courtesy Martin Spetz)

Gianpiero Moretti stands alongside his 333 SP #004 at Road Atlanta. (Courtesy Martin Spetz)

just one 333 SP in the race. This one, driven by Moretti and Salazar, proved more reliable, seeing off the challenge of Dale's Spice HC94-Oldsmobile to win the race by a minute. The Moretti/Salazar 333 SP covered 272 miles at an average speed of 91.25mph, and established the car as a contender for the Manufacturers' Championship.

Indianapolis Raceway Park, Indiana, July 10

Only 13 cars turned up to Indianapolis Raceway, a challenging 2.5-mile circuit with 15 turns. Qualifying resulted in Salazar again taking pole position; Jeremy Dale secured the second slot, closely followed by Andy Evans and Fermin Velez in the second 333 SP, #003. Absent from this race was the Baldi/Cochran car, after its problematic outing at Watkins Glen.

At the drop of the green flag, Dale's Spice HC94-Oldsmobile took the lead, with Salazar close behind, pulling away from Evans in third slot, and Weaver in fourth. Halfway through the two-hour race, Salazar captured the lead and handed the car over to Moretti for the final stint. Moretti maintained his lead whilst, behind him, Velez passed Weaver for second place. Velez had taken over the car from Evans and set his sights on catching Moretti, but time ran out with Velez just eight seconds adrift.

For Moretti, this was his third consecutive victory in #004, but he generously acclaimed Salazar's contribution: "Eliseo really won the race; all I did was drive the car to the victory circle and park it." Although understating his own part, it was clear that his belief that the car should be made and for Ferrari to return to sports prototype racing had been completely vindicated.

Laguna Seca, Monterey, California, July 24

The teams running the Ferrari 333 SPs approached the Laguna Seca race with confidence. By now, minor alterations were noticeable on the cars as each Ferrari team vied for supremacy. Between them, they had worked the car up to

third in the Manufacturers' Championship point standings; this despite missing the Daytona and Sebring races at the beginning of the season. It therefore came as some surprise when, for the first time since Road Atlanta, the 333 SP failed to make pole position on the grid. That position was claimed by Wayne Taylor's Spice HC94-Oldsmobile, ahead of Salazar, Dale in the other Spice HC94-Oldsmobile, Cochran, Velez and Weaver's Spice DR3-Ferrari.

Sunday's race started with Taylor's Spice HC94-Oldsmobile driven by co-driver Andy Wallace pulling out a sizeable lead over Salazar. Things stayed that way for the first hour. At that point, Wallace went into the pits, with an engine problem that eventually put the car out of the race. Salazar took over the lead, but was soon passed by Velez, and the two of them both entertained and deafened the crowd as they passed the lead of the race back and forth; the continuous shriek of the engines intensified by the natural bowl in which the track sat. The final move came ten minutes from the end, when Velez nudged his way ahead, giving him and co-driver Evans their first victory of the season. The car averaged 90.6mph, and finished just seven seconds ahead of second-placed Salazar.

With only two races left in the season, the WSC Manufacturers' Championship had come down to the wire, with Ferrari now tied with Oldsmobile for the honours.

Portland International Raceway, Oregon, August 8

Oldsmobile's seemingly unassailable position in the WSC Manufacturers' Championship had dwindled to nothing. It responded to the challenge from the Ferrari by fielding three cars at Portland.

Qualifying resulted in an all-Oldsmobile front row with the Velez/Evans 333 SP #003 in third slot. The Moretti/Salazar 333 SP #004 was relegated to the rear of the 15-car grid, due to tyre changes from their qualifying rubber.

The race started with Wallace pulling out a good lead over the field, Evans in second place and Moretti fourth. The first round of pit stops saw the running order unchanged, until the officials penalised Velez for speeding in the pit lane. They called him in for a stop-and-go penalty, costing him precious time. Meanwhile Salazar had taken over from Moretti and, despite an apparent lack of power, was making a concerted effort to catch and pass race leader, now Jeremy Dale.

Velez, determined to make up lost time, was scything back through the field, only to have disaster strike: the Ferrari engine coughed and momentarily slowed the car, and Hugh Fuller's Spice-Oldsmobile had nowhere to go but into its rear. Both cars limped back to the pits. The 333 SP was too badly damaged to continue.

This left Salazar with the job of restoring Ferrari's pride, but his efforts were hampered by heavy rain, and the latter stages of the race were impeded by several yellow and red flags. The race ended ten minutes early; Jeremy Dale's Spice HC94-Oldsmobile declared the winner after 75 laps, with Salazar 11 seconds adrift in second place.

Phoenix International Raceway, Phoenix, Arizona, October 1

The facts were quite simple. A Ferrari 333 SP had to win the race at Phoenix in order for the Marque to win the WSC Manufacturers' Championship. The race was started in the evening under floodlights on a tight 1.5-mile track, and attracted a grid of 18 cars.

Jeremy Dale's Spice HC94-Oldsmobile was in pole, pursued by the Ferraris of Cochran, Evans and Moretti, and the Spice DR3-Ferrari of Weaver.

The race commenced. Dale immediately took the lead, followed by Cochran and Weaver, with Evans and Moretti vying for fourth. So intense was the battle between Weaver and Cochran, that they traded places several times over the course of ten laps. Then a Tiga-Buick stalled at turn two, followed by a a flurry of yellow flags. While some drivers took advantage of the situation to make their pit stops, Cochran was forced to stay out and complete a slow-paced lap. By the time he pitted, he found himself at the back of the pack; added to which, his pit crew made a mess of the

stop, losing Cochran even more time. Not in the best frame of mind, he returned to the track, but his over-aggressive style of driving quickly caused his tyres to wear away, and he retired 20 laps from the end of the race.

At the same time, while the final pit stops were being made, Velez managed to wrestle the race lead away from Dale. He had begun to build a lead over Dale, when disaster struck; an alternator wire shook loose on the Ferrari, causing total headlight failure. Velez was shown the black flag and retired to the pits. He was not allowed back onto the track without lights. While it sought to repair the damage, the team watched its championship hopes dwindle in despair as the final laps ticked by. By the time Salazar came out

Eliseo Salazar Valenzuela

Born in Chile in 1954, Eliseo Salazar Valenzuela participated in 37 F1 GPs before turning to sports cars in 1988. He joined the Momo team in 1994, and competed in the IMSA series for a year, before racing in the Indy Car World series.

Eliseo Salazar Valenzuela.
(Courtesy IMRRC Watkins Glen)

Heading to the grid for the start of the race at Laguna Seca, Salazar leaving the heavy work to his pit crew. (Courtesy Gary Horsikorta De Vita Collection)

The grid for the start of the race at Laguna Seca, with Cochran on the front row and Evans on row two (Courtesy Gary Horsikorta De Vita Collection)

Salazar coming out of turn nine at Laguna Seca, driving #004. (Courtesy Gary Horsikorta SFR/ De Vita Collection)

Jay Cochran is chased round turn nine at Laguna Seca by the Evans/Velez car that went on to win the race. (Courtesy Gary Horsikorta SFR/ De Vita Collection)

of the pits, he was 44 seconds adrift. The chequered flag came down on Dale's car, giving Oldsmobile the WSC Manufacturers' Championship for 1994.

Whilst the 333 SPs had all come from the same source, and each had factory support, it was unfortunate that the teams running the cars failed to communicate with one another throughout the season. As a consequence, they did not form a strategy that would see the Ferrari topple the Oldsmobile in the Manufacturers' Championship. It was a case of missed opportunities.

IMSA World Sports Car Championship

Date	Race venue	No	Chassis	Entrant	Drivers	Result
17.4.94	Road Atlanta 2hr	50	005	Euromotorsport	Cochran J	1
		30	004	Momo	Moretti G/Salazar E	2
		3	003	Scandia	Bentley R/Evans A	5
		5	002	Euromotorsport	Baldi M	dnf
30.5.94	Lime Rock 2hr	30	004	Momo	Salazar E/Moretti G	1
		50	005	Euromotorsport	Cochran J	2
		3	003	Scandia	Evans A/Morgan C	3
		5	002	Euromotorsport	Baldi M	dnf
26.6.94	Watkins Glen 3hr	30	004	Momo	Salazar E/Moretti G	1
		3	003	Scandia	Evans A/Cheever E	dnf
		50	005	Scandia	Baldi M/Cochran J	dnf
10.7.94	Indianapolis 2hr	30	004	Momo	Salazar E/Moretti G	1
		3	003	Scandia	Evans A/Velez F	2
		50	005	Euromotorsport	Cochran J	dna
24.7.94	Laguna Seca 2hr	3	003	Scandia	Evans A/Velez F	1
		30	004	Momo	Salazar E	2
		50	002	Euromotorsport	Cochran J/Spence R	4
7.8.94	Portland 2hr	30	004	Momo	Moretti G/Salazar E	2
		3	003	Scandia	Evans A/Velez F	10
1.10.94	Phoenix 2hr	30	004	Momo	Moretti G/Salazar E	2
		3	003	Scandia	Evans A/Velez F	6
		50	005	Euromotorsport	Cochran J	8 nr
		5	002	Euromotorsport	Cochran J	dna

1995 – Ferrari wins the IMSA World Sports Car Championship

The plan for 1995 was simple: to win the ISMA WSC Championship. 1995 also saw the 333 SP race in Europe for the first time, at Le Mans and Jarama. Dallara produced a new batch of 333 SPs for the 1995 season, to join the existing ones. The new model incorporated a few visual bodywork changes. The teams would also add their own minor alterations.

Wayne Taylor joined the Scandia team, after agreement with Moretti that his car would carry the Danka & Konica sponsorship logos, alongside the Momo identification.

America

Daytona International Raceway, Daytona Beach, Florida, February 5

The 24-hour race at Daytona tested the durability of the Ferrari to the limit. The previous year's sprints had proved that the car was quick and fairly reliable, but, to win the major titles, the car had to prove itself at another level. Two cars were entered by the Scandia Team, one by Euromotorsport and one for the Momo team, which also brought a spare car. Scandia had taken advantage of the IMSA rules to limit engine revs to 10,500 in its two cars; but each car could drop 100 pounds from from its minimum weight. In theory the reduction in weight would compensate the power reduction from the engine but should ensure longer engine life as it was not being revved to its maximum ability.

At the practice session, the Ferraris shone; quick enough for Velez and Baldi to claim front row with their updated cars, with the other two 333 SPs, driven by

Taylor and Sigala, further down the grid in third and fifth respectively

Within a couple of hours, all four of the 333 SPs were in front, running first to fourth, but as dusk approached their luck changed.

The Momo 333 SP, #011, encountered problems when the titanium valves began to leak and the engine became difficult to start after pit stops. Then gearbox, clutch and throttle problems kept the Euromotorsport entry pit-bound for far too long to mount a challenge for the lead; but at least the car lasted the course, finishing in a respectable eighth

The Momo entry #011 on the Daytona banking before encountering engine problems that put the Ferrari out of the race. (Courtesy Jerry McDermott)

place. No such luck for the Momo and Scandia cars. After starting well, the dominating Ferraris fell out of contention, one after the other, in the early hours of Sunday morning, both suffering oil pump-related engine failure.

Sebring International Raceway, Florida, March 18

Sebring was a 12-hour race. Alboreto's Ferrari took pole, proving that the car was still the quickest in the field. Alongside him on the grid was the Brix Spice-Oldsmobile, with Jeremy Dale at the wheel.

The Alboreto/Baldi car led the race, until it was forced to stop to replace a broken upright. Then the Scandia team lost Baldi, who had to leave for Italy abruptly, mid-race, because of the death of his father. Eric van de Poele alternated between driving both Scandia cars, to help out the team.

The Momo car had been near the front of the field, but then its gearbox failed and had to be replaced, putting it out of contention. The Euromotorsport entry was running well, until it ran out of fuel; further problems meant it finished in 22nd place.

Heavy rain fell throughout, stopping the race for 75 minutes at one point, but, despite the weather conditions, the last of the Ferraris, driven by Velez/Evans/van de Poele, made up for some of the bad luck. It outlasted some strong challenges from Wallace's Spice SE90-Chevrolet and Pace's Kudza DG-3-Mazda, to win the race. Alboreto steered the other Scandia to fourth.

A refuelling miscalculation at Sebring meant the Euromotorsport entry #009 finished 22nd. (Courtesy Martin Spetz)

#011 at Sebring lost part of its tail plate. It also needed a lengthy pit stop to replace the gearbox. (Courtesy Martin Spetz)

The victorious Scandia 333 SP #003 at Sebring, with Fermin Velez at the wheel. The car had a revised body in 1995. (Courtesy Martin Spetz)

22

Road Atlanta, Braselton, Georgia, April 30

Six weeks after the Sebring event came the first of the IMSA 'sprint' races. Four 333 SPs were amongst the 41 qualifiers, with Scandia electing to bring only one entry, together with one each from Momo and Euromotorsport, and an entry from the Horag-Lista team.

Velez claimed pole position, with James Weaver's Riley & Scott Mk III Ford alongside him. Weaver led from the start, followed by Velez, and Barbazza in the Euromotorsport Ferrari, #009, in third spot. On lap 14, two backmarkers collided and blocked the track in front of the fast-approaching Barbazza. He swerved onto the grass to avoid the crash, but his car slid back onto the tarmac, right in front of Dale's Spice BDG-02-Oldsmobile. The Spice struck the Ferrari broadside, breaking the Dallara-built monocoque in half. Barbazza was knocked unconscious, fractured several bones and punctured a lung, while Dale suffered massive damage to his legs. As a result, the race was red-flagged for 90 minutes.

At the restart, Velez took the lead, but lost it to Weaver during an extra-long pit stop. Meanwhile, the Horag-Lista Ferrari, #012, was trying to make headway through the

An awkward moment for the Horag-Lista 333 SP #012 as it loses adhesion at Road Atlanta. It retired after being in a collision with a Nissan 300ZX. (Courtesy Martin Spetz)

Velez and Baldi claimed the runner-up spot at Road Atlanta for the Scandia team driving 333 SP #010. (Courtesy Martin Spetz)

The unfortunate Euromotorsport entry #009 ran at Road Atlanta, but was hit by another car, and the monocoque broke in half. (Courtesy Martin Spetz)

field, but collided with a Nissan 300ZX that had pulled out to overtake another car. This incident prompted an immediate end to the race. Weaver recorded the first win for the Riley & Scott Mk III Ford, followed by Velez in the Scandia Ferrari, and Moretti in the Momo entry.

Shearwater AFB, Halifax, Nova Scotia, May 21

With the disasters of Atlanta fresh in their minds, few of the IMSA regulars ventured to the first WSC race, at Shearwater AFB in Canada.

There were only 19 cars on the start grid, headed by the Moretti/Taylor 333 SP, #011, with Ekblom's Spice BDG-02-Oldsmobile alongside him, and Mauro Baldi's 333 SP, #010, behind him. The two other Ferraris were missing; the Euromotorsport car had been destroyed at Atlanta, and the Horag-Lista car was still being repaired.

Baldi pulled away from pole, and gradually built up a lead over the pursuing pack. Leitzinger's Riley & Scott was next, but could not get within 18 seconds of the leader. Baldi won the race, followed by Leitzinger, with the Moretti/Taylor 333 SP finishing, on the same lap as the leaders, in third.

Lime Rock, Connecticut, May 29

This scenic venue was deemed too short and narrow for mixed class racing, and consequently only had 14 starters. Scandia fielded two 333 SPs, Momo one, along with the Horag-Lista car, which had now been repaired after the accident at Atlanta. 'Repaired' was an understatement, as the tub had been completely replaced, and the official designation of the car was now #012b having being completely rebuilt from the remains of #012.

The twisty circuit suited the Riley & Scott more than the Ferrari, for whilst the latter was a quicker car on the straight, the former had more power coming out of the corners, and so held the advantage.

Despite this, Taylor earned pole for the Momo 333 SP, with Weaver's Riley & Scott next to him. From the race start,

however, Weaver set the pace. He was followed by Baldi and Taylor in the early laps, but, as the tarmac became slippery, Baldi's car slid off the track and broke a tie-rod, promoting Taylor to second place.

Wayne Taylor is on his way to record a victory at Lime Rock in the 333 SP #011. (Courtesy Martin Spetz)

The final 15 minutes of the race proved crucial. Weaver put a wheel onto the grass and lost traction; Taylor passed him to take the chequered flag.

Meanwhile, the Velez/Evans car had been making steady progress back through the field and finished third, behind Weaver, with Baldi seven laps adrift in sixth, and Lienhard in the Horag-Lista a further three laps down in eighth place.

Watkins Glen International Raceway, New York State, June 24

Whilst Lime Rock was not considered a Ferrari-friendly track, Watkins Glen was definitely more suited to the car's strengths. Two 333 SPs showed up, with Moretti/Taylor for Momo and Baldi/Velez for Scandia. Between them they earned the front row of the grid, with Baldi on pole, and Moretti beside him.

Baldi took a slight lead from the start, but Moretti was instantly passed by Leitzinger's Riley & Scott, and Ekblom's Spice BDG-02-Oldsmobile. By the time the pit stops occurred, Baldi had opened up a safe lead.

However, four brief yellow-flag periods gave Taylor, in the second 333 SP, and Weaver, driving the Riley & Scott, the chance to move up close behind Velez – Taylor in second place, and Weaver in third. Then Weaver out-braked Taylor, and moved into second place. A lap later,

The race start at Watkins Glen, with two 333 SPs vying for the lead. (Courtesy IMRRC Watkins Glen)

he out-manoeuvred Velez to take the lead. As the finish approached, Velez had to slow down to conserve fuel. Unable to challenge Weaver for the win, he came in second. Taylor suffered even worse, coasting to a stop on the final lap, out of fuel and out of the running, classified fourth on race distance covered.

Sears Point Raceway, Sonoma, California, July 16

There were four Ferraris at Sears Point: two for Scandia, one each for Momo and Horag-Lista.

Once again, Mauro Baldi claimed pole, with Weaver's Riley & Scott next to him on the front row of the grid. Unusually, the outside of the track had more grip, and Baldi was left struggling for traction. Weaver, Leitzinger and Velez had all made it past him before the end of the first turn.

The Momo 333 SP, #011, driven by Taylor, had a torrid and short race, that ended on lap 20 with a split oil filter. Meanwhile, Velez overtook Leitzinger, but could make little impression on Weaver, until a pace car closed the gap for him. With just three laps left, Velez managed one last challenge on Weaver, finishing eight seconds behind him, as the chequered flag fell. Baldi took fourth spot, just behind Leitzinger, with the Horag-Lista 333 SP, #012b, fifth.

Mosport Speedway, Bowmanville, Ontario, August 13

Mosport Speedway started with two Riley & Scott cars in front; the 333 SPs of Velez and Moretti relegated to the second row. This did not deter Velez, in the Scandia Ferrari. He was first away at the start, and took the lead. Unluckily for him, however, there were several accidents among temporary chicanes installed on the track, and the consequent yellow-flag periods cut away at his advantage.

Baldi, now driving the Scandia car, managed to retain the lead, until he was black-flagged for forcing Weaver into the wall on the first turn after the straight. The stop-and-go penalty cost Baldi the race, and gave Weaver his third victory of the year. The Moretti/Taylor 333 SP, #011,

finished third, on the same lap as the winner, while the Horag-Lista entry was fifth, one lap down.

Texas World Speedway, College Station, Texas, September 10

The rivalry between the Dyson and Scandia teams intensified as the season progressed. Things came to a head at Texas World, where the drivers took to tactically blocking their rivals on the qualifying laps.

As a result, Alboreto, in one of the two Scandia Ferraris, took pole from Wallace's Riley & Scott, and Taylor in the Momo 333 SP. The prime contenders for the drivers' title, Velez and Weaver, opted not to start first, planning instead to wait, and take over the best-placed of their respective two-car teams. The second Scandia started in fourth position.

The first real change to the Ferrari engine was introduced at this race: the two Scandia cars were fitted with an experimental twin-rail fuel injection system. Velez and Alboreto both complained that it made the car more difficult to drive.

Momo's strategy for this three-hour race was to have Taylor driving solo, thus shortening the pit stops. Scandia kept to its usual practice of having co-drivers. Keeping to the plan of switching points-leader Velez with whichever of the Scandia team cars was best-placed, he took took over from Baldi, currently in third place, but, within a few laps, Velez was back in the pits with a broken gearbox. About the same time, Leitzinger's Riley & Scott made a pit stop, and Weaver jumped in the driver seat. Then disaster struck; the clutch would not engage. When the two cars eventually came back onto the track, they were both well out of the running to take points.

Meanwhile, Taylor had gained a lap on the remainder of the field. He maintained his lead to the chequered flag, with Alboreto finishing a lap down in second, ahead of Wallace, a further lap down. Momo's strategy had paid off.

While Ferrari had improved its chances in the race for WSC Championship wins, it was quid pro quo as far as the drivers' title went.

#003 could manage only seventh place at Texas World Speedway after starting second on the grid. (Courtesy Jerry McDermott)

#003 passes through the paddock at Texas World Speedway. (Courtesy Jerry McDermott)

Phoenix Raceway, Phoenix, Arizona, September 30

Phoenix was a night race in the desert. It was two hours or 200 miles, whichever came first. This shorter time meant that several teams opted to use a single driver. Scandia fielded two cars, Momo one. The Horag-Lista car was also back, having missed Texas World.

Velez earned pole position, with Weaver next to him. However, Velez made a faltering start on the pace lap, and Weaver was able to snatch an early lead. Velez took a while to pass Weaver, but then established a substantial lead, as Weaver's Riley & Scott pitted. Furthermore, Weaver lost any advantage that fresh tyres might have given him, by re-emerging into traffic. This gifted Velez a clear track, and a pressure-free pit stop.

Velez drove a faultless race to claim victory over Weaver, with the other Scandia car, driven by Baldi, claiming third spot, after overtaking Leitzinger on the final lap. The Momo car finished fifth, two laps down, while the Horag-Lista car was eighth, five laps behind the leader.

Importantly, the Velez victory meant Ferrari won the WSC Manufacturers' Championship, ahead of Ford, and Oldsmobile. It was now up to Velez to see if he could claim the drivers' title, in the final race at New Orleans.

New Orleans, Louisiana, October 8

The course in New Orleans was a street circuit, built around the city's Convention Centre; a course that was thought to give the Riley & Scott chassis setup an advantage.

The Riley & Scott's overall performance had improved in leaps and bounds during the season, and, together with the torque produced from the Ford V-8 engine, had provided more than enough competition for the expensive 333 SPs.

Weaver was in pole on the bumpy course; alongside him was Ross Bentley in an Oldsmobile-powered Riley & Scott Mk III. The second row of the grid was taken by

Taylor in the Momo 333 SP, #011, and Velez in the Scandia 333 SP, #003.

Baldi, never at ease on confined street circuits, had qualified in a lowly 20th place. With the WSC Manufacturers' Championship secured, a 'safety first' approach was adopted by the Scandia team, to nurse home Velez to win the Drivers' Championship. No heroics were needed; just a steady drive into fourth would do the job.

Unfortunately, the concrete barrier surrounds played their part in proceedings: cars clipped them, and several yellow-flag laps kept the lead cars together. The Ferraris couldn't, or didn't, challenge the Riley & Scotts. Weaver claimed victory, followed by Leitzinger in the second Riley & Scott, with Baldi's 333 SP third. Velez, doing just what was required of him, finished fourth to claim the WSC driver's crown.

Europe

Le Mans, June 18

The 333 SP's introduction to the 24-hour race at Le Mans was not a happy one. Ferrari reluctantly supplied endurance engines for Le Mans to an insistent Euromotorsport team, concerned that the engines had not been developed sufficiently for this highly prestigious event. Ferrari told Euromotorsport that it would not support the project in its usual manner; it did not want an embarrassing repeat of the Daytona experience, at such a high-profile race. Its reluctance to participate led to speculation that it supplied a 'lame engine' to the Euromotorsport team – an accusation firmly denied by Ferrari.

The 333 SP was one of two IMSA spec cars to compete in the WSC class, and it arrived at the race fitted with an incorrect rev limiter. After some heated discussions between the Euromotorsport team and the organisers, the 333 SP #002 was allowed to qualify. In the event, this decision was irrelevant, as the car, driven by Sigala, managed just seven circuits before the motor failed, and it was left stranded at Arnage.

Fermin Velez

Fermin Velez was born in Spain in 1959. As a sports car driver, he was the two-time winner of the Sebring 12-hour race in a 333 SP while driving for Andy Evans' Scandia team, and was also two-time WSC Group C2 champion.

Fermin Velez.
(Courtesy IMRRC
Watkins Glen)

The driver line-up for the Euromotorsport entry at Le Mans. The team recruited Rene Arnoux for this race, a race Ferrari would have preferred not to be involved with this year. (Courtesy Peter Collins)

The Euromotorsport entry #002 at Le Mans before retiring after just seven laps had been completed. (Courtesy Peter Collins)

Fredy Lienhard

Fredy Lienhard was born in Switzerland in 1947. He moved to sports car racing from Formula Vee and Formula Two. He acquired a 333 SP in 1995 and competed in the European Sports Car Championship and ISMA Championships and later in the American Le Mans series.

Fredy Lienhard. (Courtesy IMRRC Watkins Glen)

Jarama Circuit, Madrid, November 5

Following an eventful time in the IMSA series Fredy Leinhard, founder of Lista Racing in the 1970s, decided to ship his car to Europe for the final race of the ISRS held at Jarama, a race, a race where a varied selection of classes turned up, with chassis 012b. After qualifying ninth on the grid of just 13 cars, he clawed his way up to finish sixth in the 40-lap race. His Ferrari was two minutes 32 seconds behind the winner, Ranieri Randaccio, driving a Fondmetal FG01-Ford Cam-Am car.

IMSA World Sports Car Championship

Date	Race venue	No	Chassis	Entrant	Drivers	Result
5.2.95	Daytona 24hr	50	009	Euromotorsport	Brancatelli G/Sigala M/Julian E/Barbazza F	8
		30*	011	Momo	Moretti G/Taylor W/Salazar E/Theys D	dnf
		3*	003	Scandia	Velez F/Evans A/Gentilozzi P/van de Poele E	dnf
		33*	010	Scandia	Baldi M/Alboreto M/Johansson S	dnf
		30T	004	Momo	–	dnr
18.3.95	Sebring 12hr	3	003	Scandia	Velez F/Evans A/van de Poele E	1
		33	010	Scandia	Baldi M/Alboreto M/van de Poele E	4
		50	009	Euromotorsport	Barbazza F/Julian E/Sigala M	22
		30	011	Momo	Moretti G/Taylor W/Theys D	34
30.4.95	Road Atlanta 3hr	3	010	Scandia	Velez F/Baldi M	2
		30	011	Momo	Moretti G/Taylor W	3
		27*	012	Horag-Lista	Theys D/Lienhard F	dnf
		50*	009	Euromotorsport	Barbazza F/Cochran J/Sigala M	dnf
21.5.95	Halifax 3hr	3	010	Scandia	Baldi M/Velez F	1
		30	011	Momo	Moretti G/Taylor W	3
29.5.95	Lime Rock	30	011	Momo	Taylor W	1
		3	003	Scandia	Velez F/Evans A	3
		33	010	Scandia	Baldi M	6
		27	012b	Horag-Lista	Lienhard F/Loessig J	8
24.6.95	Watkins Glen 3hr	3	010	Scandia	Baldi M/Velez F	2
		33	011	Momo	Moretti G/Taylor W	4
16.7.95	Sears Point	3	003	Scandia	Velez F	2
		33	010	Scandia	Baldi M	4
		27	012b	Horag-Lista	Theys D/Lienhard F	5
		30*	011	Momo	Taylor W/Moretti G	dnf

Date	Race venue	No	Chassis	Entrant	Drivers	Result
13.8.95	Mosport 3hr	3	010	Scandia	Velez F/Baldi M	2
		30	011	Momo	Moretti G/Taylor W	3
		27	012b	Horag-Lista	Theys D/Lienhard F	5
10.9.95	Texas World 3hr	30	011	Momo	Taylor W	1
		33	010	Scandia	Alboreto M	2
		3	003	Scandia	Baldi M/Velez F	24
30.9.95	Phoenix 2hr	3	003	Scandia	Velez F	1
		33	010	Scandia	Baldi M	3
		30	011	Momo	Moretti G/Taylor W	5
		27	012b	Horag-Lista	Lienhard F/Theys D	8
8.10.95	New Orleans	30	011	Momo	Taylor W	3
		3	003	Scandia	Velez F	4
		33	010	Scandia	Baldi M	6
		27	012b	Horag-Lista	Lienhard F/Theys D	dna

*not running at the finish of the race

Le Mans

Date	Race venue	No	Chassis	Entrant	Drivers	Result
18.6.95	Le Mans 24hr	1	002	Euromotorsport	Sigala M/Cochran J/Arnoux R	dnf
		2	009	J F America	-	dns

International Sports Racing Series

Date	Race venue	No	Chassis	Entrant	Drivers	Result
5.11.95	Jarama	53	012b	Horag Hotz	Lienhard F	6

1996 – Oldsmobile takes revenge

The involvement of the 333 SP in sports car racing was more subdued in 1996. Momo, Scandia and, later on, Landshark, mainly fielded just one car each at the different rounds of the WSC Championships. Conversely, Riley & Scott's success saw a growing number of teams run its cars, some with Ford engines, others Oldsmobile. Lienhard's 333 SP started the season independently, but he failed to find enough sponsorship, and he joined Moretti's operation in May, running under the Landshark banner. Meanwhile, Scandia reduced its entries to one car per race, largely due to its conflicting interests with single-seat racing. (Scandia had started running a Formula 5000 car, and it was costing them a lot of money.) Euromotorsport abandoned the 333 SP altogether, after its spat with Ferrari during the previous season, and was running an Osella PA20 instead.

America

Daytona International Raceway, Daytona Beach, Florida, February 4

There were four 333 SP entries to the Daytona 24-hour race; but only two made it to the start grid, one entered by the Momo team, the other by Scandia. Both cars sported new aerodynamic body side panels, but the Momo car had a 1994 nose. A second Momo team car was brought to Daytona, but was not funded, so did not race.

The two teams had very different luck during the race. Early on, Baldi spun the Scandia 333 SP, #003, damaging the front suspension. A few hours later, the same thing happened to his co-driver, Velez. Velez's theory was that oil

had spilled onto the tyres from somewhere in the engine bay, but no evidence of that was found when the car was inspected in the pits. Bewilderment turned to anger and arguments in the pit, as the car was wheeled away, after covering just 106 laps.

It was a different story for Momo. Bob Wollek took pole, and then maintained a front-running position for most of the race. However, with less than two hours to go before the end of the race, the car's exhaust pipe broke, not once, but twice, costing it eight laps' worth of time. The delay

Momo entered #003 for the Daytona 24-hour race, finishing in second place. (Courtesy Jerry McDermott)

gave Wayne Taylor's Riley & Scott the lead, and the Ferrari's old adversary went on to win the race, with the 333 SP still managing to finish in a highly commendable second place, four laps down on the leader.

Sebring International Raceway, Florida, March 17

The 333 SP built on its success at Daytona with a qualifying performance at Sebring that saw Max Papis, driving for Momo, in pole position, with Scandia's Alboreto alongside him. Taylor's Riley & Scott Oldsmobile was on the second row.

The race settled down, with the Momo 333 SP, #004, leading at the fifth hour, and Taylor's Riley & Scott, and Baldi's Scandia 333 SP, the only other cars in contention to win the race. It set the pattern for the remainder of the race. The lead changed hands constantly between the three cars, depending on who was taking a pit stop at the time.

The Momo and Landshark Ferraris standing in the paddock area at Road Atlanta.
(Courtesy Martin Spetz)

Preparation of the Momo/Landshark 333 SPs in the paddock at Road Atlanta for the race ahead was an important and methodical job. (Courtesy Martin Spetz)

The Ferrari power unit in #004.
(Courtesy Martin Spetz)

Shattering the tranquil scene, Moretti and
Papis drove #004 to victory at Road Atlanta.
(Courtesy Martin Spetz)

The Ferrari 333 SP speeding
to victory at Road Atlanta.
(Courtesy Martin Spetz)

Gerry Jackson made an unscheduled stop out on the track during practice at Road Atlanta.
(Courtesy Martin Spetz)

As the end approached, Baldi was leading, with Taylor close on his heels. Going into one of the banked bends, Baldi went to cut underneath a slower Porsche, but the Porsche came down the banking and collided with Baldi. The damage forced Baldi into the pits and cost him a four-lap delay. This allowed Taylor to clinch victory. Baldi finished second, ahead of the Momo in third. It proved to be an expensive collision for Baldi, as Scandia team boss Andy Evans blamed him for the mistake and fired him on the spot.

Road Atlanta, Braselton, Georgia, April 21

After the catastrophic crashes at Atlanta the previous year, IMSA reviewed the class requirements for the 1996 race. This resulted in only GTS-1s running with the WSC cars, reducing the field to 26.

The Momo and Landshark 333 SPs turned up, but Scandia missed the race in favour of single-seat racing.

The long straights at Atlanta favoured the Ferrari chassis, and Papis, driving for Momo, and Didier Theys, for Landshark, confirmed their advantage by qualifying for the front row. One of their main rivals, James Weaver, in his Riley & Scott Oldsmobile, blew an engine in practice and had to start the race at the back of the field.

At the race start, Theys took the lead, with Moretti in the Momo Ferrari dropping back to third, behind James Taylor's car, which had cut through the field at a tremendous pace. Moretti pitted early to swap places with Papis. Papis drove a series of stunning laps, giving himself an unassailable lead, and taking the chequered flag, ahead of Taylor, and Bentley's Riley & Scott Oldsmobile. Theys came in fourth, five laps adrift of the adrift of the winner, driving the Landshark 333 SP, #011.

Texas World Speedway, College Station, Texas, May 5

One week prior to the Texas World race Landshark decided to lease #011 to Gary Jackson, a wealthy individual who had already driven the car at Road Atlanta. Preparation and maintenance of the car remained the responsibility of the Momo team.

Two factors, heat and tyres, played a major part in the outcome of the 500-mile race at Texas World. Taylor's Riley & Scott Oldsmobile sat on pole, with the Papis/Moretti 333 SP, #004, next to him, while the Landshark 333 SP was on the third row of the grid.

Although Papis was first away, the Dyson team Riley & Scott Oldsmobile driven by John Paul Jr took an early lead after starting from third place on the grid. Taylor's tyres were too soft for the heat, and he struggled to keep up with the lead cars.

Papis also had tyre problems, but of a more serious nature. His right front tyre disintegrated just as he was driving along the front straight at full speed. He managed

The winning 333 SP #004 in the paddock at Lime Rock. Visual changes to the car from the previous year included smoother body work. (Courtesy Andrew Hartwell)

to limp back to the pits on three wheels, but his slow-in lap, and the resultant damage, relegated the car to seventh place. Theys/Jackson in the Landshark 333 SP also had some handling problems, and managed only fourth.

Massimiliano (Max) Papis

Massimiliano (Max) Papis was born in Italy in 1969. He competed in Formula One and Champ Car before moving to sports car racing, joining the Momo team and competing in the IMSA WSC championship.

Massimiliano (Max) Papis. (Courtesy Andrew Hartwell)

Lime Rock, Connecticut, May 27

The fastest qualifier at Lime Rock was Landshark's 333 SP, driven by Theys, but the Landshark team had mistakenly fitted the car with endurance racing wing plates, which made the car too long for the race, so Theys was relegated to the back row of the grid. This meant James Weaver's Riley & Scott Oldsmobile, and the Momo 333 SP took the front row.

Moretti had a poor start, as he had to pit on the pace lap with a loose wheel. He rejoined the rear of the pack, joining Theys in the other 333 SP. A rare sight indeed!

Theys wasted no time in cutting through the field to trail the Weaver and Leitzinger Riley & Scott cars, but Moretti found it more difficult, and was a lap down on the leaders, when he handed the car over to Papis.

A yellow flag gave Papis the opportunity to catch the leading group, and a controversial overtaking move that coincided with yellow flags being waved put Papis into second place. In retrospect, to complete his overtaking move was possibly the safest option at the time, as to pull out of the manoeuvre would have been dangerous. With ten laps to go, Papis chased down Weaver, and, on the final lap, found a way past him to snatch a dramatic victory, a mere half-second ahead of his rival. The Theys/Lienhard 333 SP finished fifth, behind three Riley & Scott cars, after a spin and stall, less than 15 minutes from the end of the race, cost Leinhard a potential second place finish.

Watkins Glen Raceway, New York State, June 9

Following several years of shorter lengths, the six-hour race was reintroduced at Watkins Glen. The Moretti/Papis car claimed pole, with Andy Wallace's Riley & Scott Ford next to him, and the Landshark 333 SP, #011, on the second row.

From the off, Papis lost the lead to Wallace, and Weaver, also driving a Riley & Scott, but he was content to sit back in third, and see how things unfolded ahead of him. He dropped back even further, when an electrics cover flew off his car and obstructed his vision.

The first pit stops shuffled the pack. Moretti took over from Papis and moved back up to third. At the second pit stop, Papis re-entered the fray, quickly passing Weaver and then Leitzinger to take the lead. Subsequent pit stops and yellow-flag periods shuffled the pack again, and, with only 20 minutes to go, Papis found himself back in third, behind Taylor and Leitzinger.

With nothing to lose, Papis drove his Ferrari to the limit, storming past Taylor and Leitzinger to clinch his third win of the season. The Landshark entry had a steady, if unspectacular, time, finishing in a solid fifth place behind three Riley & Scott cars.

Sears Point Raceway, Sonoma, California, July 14

For the first time in six months, a third 333 SP took to the grid for the IMSA race series. This was the Scandia entry, with Velez and Evans doing the driving. Leitzinger, in a Riley & Scott Oldsmobile, earned pole, with Momo 333 SP rival Papis second, ahead of Taylor's Riley & Scott.

Papis' co-driver, Moretti, was slow off the line, gifting Leitzinger a comfortable lead. Further down the field, Evans

The Momo/Landshark entry was driven to a fifth place finish at Sears Point by Lienhard and Theys. (Courtesy Gary Horskorta, SFR/De Vito Collection)

was struggling with an ill-handling and misfiring 333 SP – the Scandia was forced to retire with electrical problems, after covering just 23 laps.

The field bunched up following a yellow-flag period, caused by Dan Clark rolling his Riley & Scott at Turn Six. This resulted in Papis being in contention for a top-three finish position. That was the way it stayed until, with two laps to go, John Paul's Riley & Scott Ford coasted to a stop, out of fuel. This left Papis in second and gaining fast on Taylor. It was a nail-biting finish, with Papis crossing the line just 0.198 seconds behind Taylor. The Landshark Ferrari finished fifth again, two laps down on the race winner.

Mosport Speedway, Bowmanville, Ontario, August 25

Mosport Speedway had been a chaotic race the previous year, with numerous accidents along the temporary chicanes. A different layout to the circuit for 1996 did not make it any better. There were frequent slow laps so that the scattered tyres forming the temporary barrier at Turn Seven could be reassembled.

Again, three Ferraris turned up. The Landshark entry had now been formally incorporated into the Momo set-up. Jackson and Lienhard had gone. Papis, Moretti and Theys alternated between the two Momo cars for the three-hour race.

One of their cars, #004, had been badly damaged while testing at Mosport, and was rebuilt using a temporary tub from #005, provided by Ferrari North America.

Scandia boss Andy Evans had been busy recruiting. He was not after driver talent so much as moneyed drivers, and Brazilian banker Antonio Hermann had paid for the privilege of partnering Velez for the remainder of the season.

The Momo Ferraris made front row, but it was Leitzinger's Riley & Scott that quickly took the lead. Then, just six minutes into the race, came the first caution period under yellow flags, in order to allow repairs to be made to the temporary chicanes. At the restart, Velez jumped ahead. He consolidated his lead while Leitzinger and Theys pitted, but then had to relinquish his drive to Hermann, who dropped four places within two laps.

The final yellow flag came 30 minutes before the end of the race. Paul took over the lead in his Riley & Scott, setting the fastest lap of the race as he pulled away from the Ferraris. Papis made a last lap charge, and he and Paul were inseparable as they approached the final bend. Paul took a gamble, diving inside at Turn 10. It paid off – he won by a whisker, 0.189 seconds ahead of Paul. The other Momo car, with Theys driving, finished third. Velez recovered some lost ground in the Scandia Ferrari to finish fifth, a lap down on the race winner.

Dallas, Texas, September 1

At just two hours' duration, this street race was classified as a sprint for the WSC entries. Practice went terribly for Papis – he hit a wall, eliminating his car from the race. He was a single point behind Wayne Taylor in the WSC Drivers' Championship, and now had to co-drive the Theys car to have any chance of gaining more points.

The Scandia 333 SP was also there, with Salazar at the wheel, making only his second appearance of the season with the team. He immediately made an impact, claiming pole position for the race. Paul was alongside him on the grid.

From the start, Paul pulled away from Salazar, with Leitzinger in third. Behind Leitzinger was Papis, though not for long as disaster struck – the gearbox on his Ferrari disintegrated, putting him out of the race on the second lap. No points for Papis, who virtually handed the Drivers' Championship to Taylor – who only needed was to finish inside the top three places to secure the title.

Salazar was trading places at the front with Leitzinger and Paul, until, with 12 laps left, Salazar had to pit with a badly-cut tyre, re-entering the race in third spot. Determined to make up places, Salazar pushed the Ferrari to the limit, only to tangle with Rob Morgan's Cutlass-Oldsmobile, and end up parked against the wall. Taylor finished second, behind Leitzinger, all but wrapping up the drivers' title. The

Scandia Ferrari was classified as finishing fourth on distance covered when the chequered flag fell.

Daytona International Raceway, Daytona Beach, Florida, October 6

The WSC party began at the Daytona 24-hour race in February, and now ended the season at the same venue in October for the three-hour race.

A large field of 56 cars started in front of a handful of spectators – tropical storm Josephine had hit Florida, and few people wanted to leave home.

While Taylor had as good as secured the drivers' title, the Manufacturers' Championship was still in the balance between Oldsmobile and Ferrari. Ford had performed well in the latter stages of the season, but was out of contention for the title. Pole position was taken by Leitzinger's Riley & Scott Mk III Ford, the Moretti/Papis Momo 333 SP alongside, following a wet practice session.

It was a wet start, and intermittent rain throughout the race resulted in slower-than-usual times being recorded.

The Scandia entry #003 failed to finish at Le Mans after Andy Evans ploughed into a gravel trap at high speed. (Courtesy Paul Kooyman)

Paul Jr immediately pulled ahead of Andy Wallace, both driving Riley & Scott Mk III Fords. Moretti was on intermediate tyres, starting cautiously and hampering the cars behind with spray, letting the pair of Riley & Scotts build up a substantial lead in the first few laps. Meanwhile, Hermann spun the Scandia Ferrari – Taylor's car was drowned out by the spray, forcing its early retirement from the race.

For a while, Paul dominated the race. Salazar was moving up the field, having taken over from Hermann, but was still a lap down. The other two Ferraris were near the front – Papis bringing the Ferrari back into contention with a series of quick laps following Moretti's slow start, while Theys was able to stay on the pace to challenge the leading Riley & Scott. Theys took the lead just as another

downpour hit the track, and he aquaplaned trying to enter the pits. The rain was causing havoc – Salazar spun his Ferrari, as did Taylor. Leitzinger managed to stay on track and win the race, while Theys recovered to take second, and Taylor came third. The finishing order meant that Ferrari and Oldsmobile were tied on points, but Oldsmobile took the Championship, based on having more victories during the season.

Europe

Le Mans, June 16
After missing the majority of IMSA races in America, the Scandia team focused its attention on the Le Mans 24-hour race.

The Ferrari 333 SP #010 in action at Le Mans. (Courtesy Peter Collins)

The second Scandia car, entered under the 'Racing for Belgium' banner, also failed to finish. (Courtesy Paul Kooyman)

The Ferrari factory was far less hostile to the idea of its cars entering the 24-hour event than it had been the year before, as the 333 SP had now proved that it could last the distance.

Dallara made some modifications to the two Scandia entries. There was a thinner front airfoil and a single plane rear wing, mounted further back than when the cars ran in America. In addition, more attention had been paid to air cooling of the engine and brakes.

One car was driven by Evans, Velez and Gentilozzi, while the second car became the 'Racing for Belgium' entry of Eric van de Poele, Eric Bachelart and Marc Goosens, with Tony Southgate managing of the team. Unfortunately, Evans made a mistake in the opening hour of the race, and ploughed into the gravel trap at Mulsanne. It took about 15 minutes to dig the 333 SP #003 out, and to complete his

misery, it ran out of fuel on the circuit after just 31 laps. The other Ferrari crept up the running order during the night, and was lying fifth after 12 hours, but then developed gearbox trouble which slowed its progress. Rushing to make up for lost time after a driver change, Bachelart left the pits on cold tyres and spun into the barriers at the Dunlop Bridge. The car had completed 208 laps when the incident occurred, ending the race for the 'Racing for Belgium' team.

Most, August 4

The Horag-Hotz team travelled to Most for a round of the Interserie races. The race was held in two heats, the results being added together to determine the winner.

After qualifying in tenth place, with Markus Hotz driving, the team pulled out of the race and did not appear on the start grid of either heat.

IMSA World Sports Car Championship

Date	Race venue	No	Chassis	Entrant	Drivers	Result
4.2.96	Daytona 24hr	30	004	Momo	Moretti G/Wollek/Theys D/Papis M	2
		31	011	Momo	Auberlen W/Hubman T/Morton J/Papis M/Moretti G	dns
		3	003	Scandia	Baldi M/Alboreto M/Velez F	62
		23	010	Scandia	Evans A/Baldi M/Alboreto M/Velez F	dna
17.3 96	Sebring 12hr	3		Scandia	Evans A/Baldi M/Alboreto M	2
		30	004	Momo	Moretti G/Papis M/Theys D	3
21.4.96	Road Atlanta	30	004	Momo	Moretti G/Papis M	1
		66	011	Landshark	Theys D/Jackson G	4
5.5.96	Texas World	66	011	Landshark	Theys D/Jackson G	4
		30	004	Momo	Moretti G/Papis M	7

Date	Race venue	No	Chassis	Entrant	Drivers	Result
27.5.96	Lime Rock	30	004	Momo	Moretti G/Papis M	1
		66	011	Landshark	Theys D/Lienhard F	5
9.6.96	Watkins Glen	30	004	Momo	Moretti G/Papis M	1
		66	011	Landshark	Lienhard F/Theys D/Jackson G	5
14.7.96	Sears Point	30	004	Momo	Moretti G/Papis M	2
		66	011	Landshark	Lienhard F/Theys D	5
		3	003	Scandia	Evans A	17nr
25.8.96	Mosport	30	004/5	Momo	Theys D/Papis M	2
		66	011	Landshark	Moretti G/Theys D	3
		3	003	Scandia	Velez F/Hermann A	5
1.9.96	Dallas	3	003	Scandia	Salazar E	4
		66	011	Landshark	Theys D	dnf
		30	004b	Momo	Papis M	dns
6.10.96	Daytona	66	011	Landshark	Theys D	2
		30	004b	Momo	Moretti G/Papis M	4
		3	003	Scandia	Hermann A/Salazar E	5

Le Mans

Date	Race venue	No	Chassis	Entrant	Drivers	Result
16.6 96	Le Mans 24hr	17	010	Equip Belge (Scandia)	van de Poele E/Bachelart E/Goosens M	dnf
		18	003	Scandia	Evans A/Velez F/Muller	dnf
		–	004	Moretti Racing	–	dna

Most

Date	Race venue	No	Chassis	Entrant	Drivers	Result
4.8.96	Most	53	012b	Horag-Hotz	Hotz M	dns

1997 – The International Sports Racing Series emerges in Europe

At the end of 1996, the IMSA changed hands – Andy Evans and Roberto Muller acquired the organisation, much to the dismay of some of the teams who participated in the race series. Andy Evans immediately stamped his authority on the competition, changing its name from IMSA to 'Professional Sports Car Racing,' not to be confused with the European Sports Racing Series.

One very noticeable, and worrying, feature of the series was the lack of spectators. Many rounds were played out before near-empty stands. NASCAR was the dominant brand name in America, and changes in several other titles in US sports and prototype racing was making it hard for the public to feel engaged.

Scandia competed in the first two races, but after the Sebring event, Evans stepped down from his entrant and driver role, instead concentrating his efforts on race administration for the PSCR. The cars were leased out, but still run by Scandia personnel. Eduardo Dibos leased #003, while Charles Morgan took charge of #004b.

In Europe, the newly-formed International Sports Racing Series had four races on their schedule. No championship points were awarded – they were being run by the organiser, John Mangoletsi, as pilot races prior to a FIA-sanctioned series beginning in 1998.

Back at the Ferrari factory, responsibility for building and maintaining the Ferrari 333 SP was transferred from Dallara to Michelotto, at the end of 1996, a decision which did not go down well with all the customer teams. Responsibility for developing and maintaining the four-litre V12 engine was given to Mauro Forghieri's Oral Engineering.

One of Michelotto's first moves was to develop a six-speed version of the transverse gearbox, but it proved to be notoriously weak, and Kevin Doran, head of the Moretti Racing team, quickly reverted to the original five-speed transmission.

Michelotto's main problem was that it had a restricted budget, and had to build a customer car that was not necessarily the best for any particular track, but that had to be a competitive privateers' prototype everywhere.

America

Daytona International Speedway, Daytona Beach, Florida, February 2

There were 80 race starters, in four different classes. This presented a real problem for the WSC cars, as they would spend much of the race overtaking the slower cars. It was rarely a problem on the banking, but the infield section was inevitably crowded, and passing safely was a constant issue.

The two Ferraris in the race had different modifications. The Moretti Racing car went with more of a compromise setup, while Scandia focused on improving downforce on the oval banking. To that end, Scandia used the same bodywork as used at Le Mans the previous year.

The Scandia 333 SP, #003, took pole, with the Moretti Racing entry alongside it. The two Riley & Scott cars were on the second row.

No one car was able to dominate proceedings in the early stages of the race – unforced errors, traffic, and

#011 finished seventh at Daytona; never in contention for honours. (Courtesy Jerry McDermott)

pit stops, ensured that the lead was constantly changing hands.

As the race progressed, Wallace's Riley & Scott went out of the race with engine failure on lap 227, and Taylor's car followed suit on lap 427, giving the Ferraris a good chance of winning.

Velez was having a frustrating time, however, as he kept having to make up time and distance each time he took the wheel, after both his co-drivers kept spinning the car. When he handed over to Charles Morgan, he was only one lap down on the leader, Leitzinger, but Morgan promptly spun, and collided with a Riley & Scott. The 333 SP came off the poorer, and didn't handle well for the remaining two hours.

Eventually, Velez was put back in the car, but it was too late to make any difference to the result. He had to concede defeat to Leitzinger, as he coaxed the oil-burning, steaming Riley & Scott to the finish line.

The Moretti Racing 333 SP was never in with a chance of winning, as, once again, money had talked louder than talent – Hermann was on the team. Hermann was just not quick enough, and the car finished in seventh place, 30 laps down on the race winner.

Sebring International Raceway, Florida, March 15

Qualifying saw Ferrari dominate the time charts, with the Velez/Dalmas Scandia on pole, and the other Scandia 333 SP next to it, driven by father and son, Charles and Rob Morgan. Emphasising its superiority, the Moretti Racing Ferrari secured third place, ahead of a group of five Riley & Scotts.

Yannick Dalmas and James Weaver had an early clash, resulting in Dalmas having to pit with a cut tyre, and, during the early hours of the race, the lead changed constantly, depending on the pit stop schedule of each leading car.

During the fifth hour, an accident halted the race for around 60 minutes. Montermini, in the Moretti Racing 333 SP, assumed the lead, but the Ferrari ran out of fuel just as it entered the pit lane, and had to be pushed into its pit slot, costing crucial time.

On lap 135, the Scandia Ferrari, driven by Charles Morgan, became the unwitting victim of Scott Sharp's Riley & Scott. Sharp's car blew an engine, and left a trail of oil on

Following a routine stop #003 leaves the pits. It finished second overall in the 24-hour race. (Courtesy Jerry McDermott)

Dibos and Auberlen drove #003, leased from the Scandia team, to fourth place at Lime Rock. (Courtesy Andrew Hartwell)

#010 was run by Moretti Racing at Lime Rock with Hermann and Montermini driving. Hermann, a banker from Brazil, had limited skill but plenty of money to buy a drive. (Courtesy Andrew Hartwell)

the circuit. Morgan's car hit the oil, spun and collided with a Porsche, leaving Morgan with a broken hand. 33 laps later, Hermann, driving the Moretti Racing 333 SP, collided with another Porsche. This sent the Ferrari into the barriers, and out of the race. Derek Bell had been scheduled to drive the Moretti Racing car, but was displaced by Hermann just before the start. The decision to replace Bell with Hermann (blamed for the collision) weighed heavily on the team.

Meanwhile at the front, the surviving Scandia 333 SP had to take on a splash of extra fuel during the final lap, but managed to cross the finish line just 16 seconds ahead of the Riley & Scott driven by James Weaver, to record a famous victory. For Johansson it was two wins in two starts at the circuit, while for Dalmas, his victory was on his first visit to Sebring.

Road Atlanta, Braselton, Georgia, April 20

Road Atlanta was the first sprint event of the season, and was also the first race without the Scandia team. Andy Evans had transferred one Ferrari 333 SP, #003, to Eduardo Dibos, who kept Fermin Velez as his lead driver, while the other car, #004b, went to Charles Morgan, and was managed by Scandia crew chief, Steve McCaughey.

Velez was on pole, with the Moretti Racing team car also at the front. Morgan's car, driven by Salazar, was on the second row.

Each of the 333 SPs started with their slower drivers, Dibos partnered with Velez, Hermann in the Moretti Ferrari, and Rob Morgan with Salazar in the CAR Services entry. Leitzinger took full advantage, and pulled into the lead in his Riley & Scott Ford, with Hermann holding second.

After the driver change-over, Montermini, in for Hermann, assumed the lead, and maintained it until the next driver change. Hermann then lost the top spot to the Forbes-Robinson/Paul Jr Riley & Scott Mk III Ford. However, it was Leitzinger who finally regained the lead to win the race. The Moretti Racing 333 SP finished third, one lap down on the winning car. The Morgan/Salazar 333 SP took fifth, while the Dibos 333 SP was down in tenth, due to a

prolonged pit stop. Things had not gone as smoothly for the CAR Services team, or for the Dibos team, as when Andy Evans was in charge of what was then the Scandia team.

Lime Rock, Connecticut, May 26

A small grid of 15 took to the track at Lime Rock. With some of the quicker Ferrari drivers unavailable due to other commitments, the front row was taken by Riley & Scott cars. The Riley & Scotts dominated the field for most of the race. Not until the latter stages, after the Riley & Scott cars encountered electrical problems, did the Moretti Racing 333 SP, #010, managed to take the lead. Montermini, having taken over from the slower Hermann, extended his lead, and won the race comfortably. The ex-Scandia cars never challenged for the top positions, finishing in fourth and sixth spots.

Watkins Glen Raceway, New York State, June 1

A field of 44 cars, of different classes, was on the grid for the start of the six-hour Watkins Glen race.

The Moretti Racing Ferrari was on pole, with Wayne Taylor's Riley & Scott next to it. Velez was on the second row, and Salazar on row three.

The race began in very wet conditions, and the first few laps ran under the caution flags. Chaos ensued when the rain stopped and cars began to pit to change tyres – too soon for some, as they ended up spinning on the wet track surface. It became the lap-scorer's worst nightmare: Montermini led the pack, helped by a prolonged yellow-flag period, when low speeds meant the cars' tyres were too cold, and yet more spun off the track.

As the weather gradually improved, some semblance of order returned. Leitzinger emerged as race leader, with Montermini second, ahead of Weaver, and Rob Morgan, the latter having struggled with his first wet outing in the powerful 333 SP.

More rain led to more problems for the drivers of the leading cars. Montermini went onto the grass, spun and

A driver change during a pit stop for the Velez/Dibos car at Watkins Glen. (Courtesy IMRRC Watkins Glen)

Pit crew duty on a wet day at Watkins Glen could be challenging, but had to be done. (Courtesy IMRRC Watkins Glen)

#003 comes into the pits for a nosecone change at Watkins Glen after one of many minor collisions on the wet track. (Courtesy IMRRC Watkins Glen)

collided with the barriers, bringing his race to an end. Meanwhile, Dibos languished in 27th place, very unhappy in the wet conditions.

Salazar took over from Rob Morgan, kept the 333 SP on the tarmac, and finished in a commendable second place – the only driver to finish on the same lap as race winner, Butch Leitzinger, in the Riley & Scott Mk III Ford.

Sears Point Raceway, Sonoma, California, July 17

The appearance on the grid of the Lienhard/Theys 333 SP had become a rare sight. The car (#016) was one of two

the Lista team owned, and had been away in Europe, competing in the ISRS races, but now it made a welcome return to America, at Sears Point Raceway.

Montermini put the Moretti Racing 333 SP on pole, with one of the other Ferraris, driven by Dibos, next to him. The Lienhard entry was on the second row, while Rob Morgan's car was back on the fifth.

Hermann started for the Moretti Racing team, and promptly launched the car up the hillside, off the exit from Turn One, lighting up the dry grass behind him into a brush fire. Out of the race on the first turn, Moretti's patience was being tested to the extreme.

Eduardo Dibos was at the wheel of #003 at Sears Point. He and Velez drove the car to a third place finish in the race. (Courtesy Martin Spetz)

#010 made a quick exit at Sears Point, going out on the first lap with Hermann at the wheel. (Courtesy Martin Spetz)

The remaining cars were eventually released from behind the pace car on lap seven, with John O'Connell's Hawk-Chevrolet taking the lead.

Elliott Forbes-Robinson's Riley & Scott took the lead, when the Hawk-Chevrolet coasted to a stop on track. At that point, Dibos pitted early, so that Velez could take up the challenge. Now in fifth, Velez could do no better than work the Ferrari up to third before the chequered flag fell. The Morgan/Salazar Ferrari followed Velez across the line, while engine problems kept the Lienhard/Theys Ferrari in a distant sixth spot, two laps down on the race winners, Wallace and Weaver in their Riley & Scott Mk III Ford.

Mosport Speedway, Bowmanville, Ontario, August 31

A field of just 13 cars turned up for the two-hour race at Mosport Speedway, four of those Ferraris. The Moretti Racing team took the Lienhard car #016 under its wing, together with its regular car #010, while the Charles Morgan and Dibos cars were also there. Their main rivals would be the five Riley & Scott cars.

Gone were the much-criticized tyre chicanes, and a bump along the back straight had been smoothed down. Ferraris dominated the start grid. Ron Fellows, standing in for Salazar, took pole position, with Montermini next to him, and Moretti behind.

At the race start, Fellows took the lead, with Leitzinger, and Taylor in close pursuit, having overtaken the slower Ferrari drivers, Hermann and Dibos. The first pit stops shuffled the pack. Leitzinger took the lead, with van de Poele's Riley & Scott Oldsmobile close behind, while the Charles Morgan/Fellows Ferrari had slipped down to fifth place.

The final pit stops followed a yellow-flag period. Velez and Morgan moved up the leader board. On the run to the chequered flag, it was the two ex-Scandia Ferraris in front, Velez ahead of Charles Morgan, and with Weaver's Riley & Scott in third.

Charles Morgan was at the wheel of #004b at Sears Point, finishing fourth overall. (Courtesy Martin Spetz)

Salazar co-drove with Charles Morgan at Sears Point. (Courtesy Martin Spetz)

With under 15 minutes to go, Velez began slowing, and informed the pits he was running out of fuel, but he was ordered to stay out by team owner, Eduardo Dibos. It turned out to be a monumental mistake by the inexperienced boss – Velez ran out of fuel two laps short of winning the race. This gave Morgan the lead, and he carefully guided his 333 SP #004b to victory. Weaver came in second. The Moretti Racing car took fourth, while the stranded Velez/Dibos car was awarded fifth spot on distance covered. The Hermann/Montermini car was well out of contention, finishing 15 laps behind the winner.

Las Vegas, Nevada, September 20

Las Vegas Motor Speedway was a new venue for the WSC cars. Intense heat melted the tarmac, scuppering everybody's preparation for the race. Practice time was minimal, and setup time was limited to the few practice laps the teams had for this night race. At least all the teams were racing in the dark on equal terms, but it did not alter the course of the race.

Clear blue sky – and a nigh empty stadium at Las Vegas. Hall and Morgan drove #004b to a fourth place finish at this track in the desert. (Courtesy Martin Spetz)

Four Ferraris turned up, Montermini's 333 SP joining pole-sitter Leitzinger on the first row. For once, the other Ferraris struggled, and were some way down the grid.

Although Montermini led the race in the early stages, a disastrously-long pit stop put him out of the running, as both Leitzinger and Taylor passed him, and pulled ahead. The Moretti Racing 333 SP did manage to hold on to third spot, with Morgan's 333 SP close behind, and Moretti's Ferrari a further lap back.

The Salazar/Dibos Ferrari #003 driven by Salazar barely troubled the lap scorers, going out with electrical trouble after only eight laps.

Pikes Peak International Raceway, September 28

One week on, and the WSC cars were at another new venue, this time in Colorado.

Andrea Montermini captured yet another pole for the Moretti Racing team, ahead of ahead of Theys in the Moretti 333 SP #010. The Dibos entry failed to show, as the previous week's electrical problems still plagued the car

Velez was at the wheel of #003 during practice at Las Vegas. Salazar drove the car in the race, but failed to finish. (Courtesy Martin Spetz)

#010, driven by Montermini and Hermann, claimed victory at Pikes Peak. (Courtesy Martin Spetz)

A routine pit stop for #004b at Pikes Peak, where the car could manage only seventh place. (Courtesy Martin Spetz)

As they had done in previous races the teams running Ferraris put their slowest drivers in at the start of the race. They soon found themselves behind Paul, Taylor and Jochamowitz, with the two Riley & Scott of Weaver and Bentley also challenging the Ferraris for track position. A quarter of the way through the race, Hermann handed over the Moretti Racing car to Montermini, and he immediately set about chasing the leading pack. He fought his way to the front, leaving Taylor and Weaver to fight for second place. A quick pit stop followed, but Montermini came out in front, to win comfortably. The other Moretti Racing entry finished fifth, but on the same lap as the winner, while Morgan's 333 SP #004b was seventh, two laps down.

Sebring International Raceway, Florida, October 18

Discontent among the teams was rife, due to the autonomous rule changes announced by race organiser Andy Evans that would equate American and European classes, and reconfigure the prize money system. The implication to the teams of these changes meant that they would have to spend money on reconfiguring the specification of their cars to European standards – more costs for no return was the teams' verdict.

So incensed was the Daytona Speedway owner, Bill France, that he joined with SCCA's Pro Racing division to announce a rival series for 1998. This would take Daytona out of Evans' 1998 schedule of events.

During qualifying, the ex-Scandia 333 SP was quickest, During qualifying the ex-Scandia 333 SP was quickest but it had undergone an engine change between qualifying and competing and had to start from the back of the grid. The front row line-up was the same as for Pikes Peak, with Montermini in pole, and Theys alongside him. Eduardo Dibos was not available to race, so Hall and Morgan rotated between the Dibos Ferrari and the other 333 SP #004b.

Once again, the Riley & Scotts out-performed the slower Ferrari drivers at the start, and it was not until the drivers changed that things improved for the 333 SP teams. Two Oldsmobile engine failures on track brought about a yellow-flag period that let the pack bunch up behind the leaders, and then it started to rain. The Moretti Racing Ferraris immediately pitted, switching to wet tyres, and gained a clear advantage over other teams that had been slower to react. The scramble of pit stops that followed, saw the Moretti Racing cars take the lead. Montermini squeezed out Theys on the final lap, and took the victory. Salazar finished fourth, with the Morgan 333 SP seventh, one lap down on the winning car.

The result saw Ferrari and Ford competing for the Manufacturers' Championship in the final round of the series.

Laguna Seca, Monterey, California, October 26

The largest field of cars for the WSC series, 21 in total, lined up for the start of the final WSC race of the season.

The start grid had a familiar look about it, Montermini on pole, Theys next to him, and Salazar on the second row in the Dibos 333 SP, #003.

At the Sebring race held in October, #003 finished fourth behind two other Ferraris. (Courtesy Martin Spetz)

With a far better start than usual, the slower of the Moretti Racing Ferrari drivers saw off the initial challenge of the Riley & Scott cars, while Salazar, in the Dibos Ferrari, took the lead, quickly creating a ten-second gap between himself and the chasing pack. The Dibos team were loath to make a change, so Salazar kept driving after the first pit stop, maintaining his comfortable lead. However, things changed at the second pit stop. Salazar pitted, and jumped out, but Velez had difficulty with the seat, and it took him a minute to secure himself in the car, allowing Leitzinger to take the lead.

As Velez fought his way back towards the front, he and Weaver collided. The Ferrari spun across the track and sustained some damage, but continued on its way. In all the confusion, Montermini slipped through into second place, while Velez recovered to finish fourth, followed one lap adrift by the other Moretti Racing 333 SP (driven by Lienhard and Theys). Morgan's car had never been on the pace, and finished five laps down on the race winner Bernd Schneider's Riley & Scott finished in tenth.

As one of the drivers of the winning Riley & Scott car, Leitzinger's success at Laguna Seca confirmed him as Drivers' Championship. The win also gave Ford the Manufacturers' Championship, six points ahead of Ferrari.

Europe

Meanwhile, in Europe, the newly-formed International Sports Racing Series had very few entries at its races, which were pilot races ahead of 1998. They were split into two classes, SR1 and SR2. SR1 was more akin to WSC, as no turbo-powered cars from class SR1 were allowed in the ISRS races.

Two European-domiciled 333 SPs were regular participants, one driven by IMSA/Sports Car regulars, Fredy Lienhard and Didier Theys, while the other one was run by long-time F40 exponent, Michel Ferte, and co-driver Adrian Campos. Before competing in the ISRS, the 333 SPs attended two other European races.

The location never fails to impress! The Moretti Racing and CAR Services 333 SPs make their way through the corkscrew at Laguna Seca. (Courtesy Martin Spetz)

Montermini and Hermann finished second at Laguna Seca driving 333 SP #010. (Courtesy Martin Spetz)

A pit stop for the Horag-Hotz 333 SP #012b, which failed to finish at Monza. (Courtesy Keith Bluemel)

Monza, March 23

The teams' first appearance in Europe was at the Monza 1000km race, during March – round one of the Challenge Endurance Italia Series. One was entered by Horag-Hotz, for Lienhard and Theys, while a second car was entered by Gianpiero Moretti (#010). After qualifying first on the grid, the Moretti-entered car finished in seventh place, while the Horag-Hotz entry, also on the first row of the grid, failed to finish the race, going out on lap 73.

Le Mans, June 15

Two Ferrari 333 SPs were entered in the Le Mans 24-hour event. The one from the Moretti Racing team had carbon fibre brakes, and had been used at Le Mans, was qualified third quickest. The other 'standard' 333 SP was from Michel Ferte.

Didier Theys

Didier Theys was born in Belgium in 1956. He was a two-time winner of the Daytona 24-hour race and a winner of the Sebring 12-hour race in a 333 SP. He became Sports Racing prototype driver champion of the Grand-Am series in 2002.

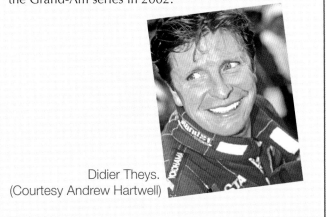

Didier Theys.
(Courtesy Andrew Hartwell)

Both cars found themselves at a distinct power disadvantage, due to new air restrictor rules that favoured the turbocharged Porsche engines. Ferte's 333 SP retired after just 18 laps with fuel system failure, but the Moretti Racing car proved more reliable and, despite several electrical problems that delayed the car in the pits, survived the full 24 hours to finish sixth, 40 laps behind the winning Porsche WSC95.

Donington Park, July 6

It was early July when the cars next made an appearance, this time at Donington Park, to attend the inaugural race of the ISRS. Only eight starters marked the occasion, among them the Horag-Hotz entry, and Michel Ferte's car (#005), but they were up against the Le Mans-winning Porsche WSC95. Ferte claimed pole, and was running well, but then had to slow down when the car developed rear-end vibration, and then ran out of fuel. This allowed the other Ferrari to claim second spot, behind the Porsche WSC95. Ferte was awarded fourth place on distance covered.

Zolder, August 3

Zolder was the next round of the ISRS, and again eight cars were on the start grid. Ferte's luck was out again – his car was misfiring, and he went out of the race after 22 laps. The Lienhard/Theys 333 SP had a much better race, driving to victory after a late duel with Jerome Policand's Courage-Porsche.

Le Mans, September 21

Only Michel Ferte's 333 SP #005 turned up for the Le Mans four-hour race, held over two heats. During the first heat, held on the Saturday evening, malfunctioning headlights hampered any progress he could make, and his car finished ten laps down. It was much more competitive during the second heat, on the Sunday, finishing second, on the same lap as the heat- and race-winner, a Courage-Porsche. Overall, the 333 SP was classified as fourth.

Jarama, November 11

The final race of the ISRS, held at Jarama, had a field of ten cars. The usual two Ferraris turned up, but Ferte's car remained in the paddock, unable to fire up. To add to the misery for the Ferrari teams, a four-car incident on the first lap put Lienhard's 333 SP #012b out of the race.

The Pilot Racing 333 SP #005, together with the impressive Pilot Racing transporter in the paddock at Le Mans. (Courtesy Peter Collins)

Professional Sports Car Racing World Sports Car Championship

Date	Race venue	No	Chassis	Entrant	Drivers	Result
2.2.97	Daytona 24hr	3	003	Scandia	Velez F/Evans A/Morgan C/Morgan R	2
		30	011	Moretti Racing	Moretti G/Hermann A/Theys D/Bell D	7
15.3.97	Sebring 12hr	3	003	Scandia	Dalmas Y/Johansson S/Velez F/Evans A	1
		30	011	Moretti Racing	Moretti G/Hermann A/Theys D/Montermini A	dnf
		43	004b	Scandia	Morgan C/Morgan R	dnf

Date	Race venue	No	Chassis	Entrant	Drivers	Result
20.4.97	Road Atlanta	30	010	Moretti Racing	Hermann A/Montermini A	3
		43	004b	C.A.R Services	Morgan C/Salazar E	5
		3	003	Dibos	Dibos E/Velez F	10
26.5.97	Lime Rock	30	010	Moretti Racing	Hermann A/Montermini A	1
		3	003	Dibos	Dibos E/Auberlen W	4
		43	004b	C.A.R.Services	Morgan C/Morgan R	6
1.6.97	Watkins Glen	43	004b	C.A.R.Services	Salazar E/Morgan C	2
		3	003	Dibos	Dibos E/Velez F	27
		30	010	Moretti Racing	Montermini A/Hermann A	31
13.7.97	Sears Point	3	003	Dibos	Dibos E/Velez F	3
		43	004b	C.A.R.Services	Salazar E/Morgan C	4
		27	016	Lista	Lienhard F/Theys D	6
		30	010	Moretti Racing	Hermann A	dnf
31.8.97	Mosport	43	004b	C.A.R.Services	Fellows R/Morgan C	1
		27	016	Moretti Racing	Moretti G/Theys D	4
		3	003	Dibos	Dibos E/Velez F	5
		30	010	Moretti Racing	Hermann A/Montermini A	9
20.9.97	Las Vegas	30	010	Moretti Racing	Montermini A/Hermann A	3
		43	004b	C.A.R.Services	Hall D/Morgan C	4
		27	016	Moretti Racing	Moretti G/Theys D	6
		3	003	Dibos	Salazar E	dnf
28.9.97	Pikes Peak	30	010	Moretti Racing	Hermann A/Montermini A	1
		27	016	MorettiRacing	Lienhard F/Theys D	5
		43	004b	C.A.R.Services	Hall R/Morgan C	7
		3	003	Dibos	Dibos E/Velez F	dna
18.10.97	Sebring	30	010	Moretti Racing	Hermann A/Montermini A	1
		27	016	Moretti Racing	Lienhard F/Theys D	2
		3	003	Dibos	Salazar E/Hall R/Morgan C	4
		43	004b	C.A.R.Services	Hall R/Morgan C	7
26.10.97	Laguna Seca	30	010	Moretti Racing	Hermann A/Montermini A	2
		3	003	Dibos	Salazar E/Velez F	4
		27	016	Moretti Racing	Lienhard F/Theys D	5
		43	004b	C.A.R. Services	Hall R/Morgan C	10

International Sports Racing Series

Date	Race venue	No	Chassis	Entrant	Drivers	Result
6.7.97	Donington	6	016	Horag Hotz	Lienhard F/Theys D	2
		8	005	Pilot Racing	Campos A/Ferte M	dnf
3.8.97	Zolder	6	012b	Horag Hotz	Lienhard F/Theys D	1
		8	005	Michel Ferte	Campos A/Ferte M	dnf
21.9.97	Le Mans	7	005	Pilot Racing	Campos A/Ferte M	4
9.11.97	Jarama	6	012b	Horag Hotz	Lienhard F/Theys D	dnf
		7	005	Pilot Racing	Campos A/Ferte M	dns

Le Mans

Date	Race venue	No	Chassis	Entrant	Drivers	Result
15.6.97	Le Mans 24hr	3	010	Moretti Racing	Theys D/Moretti G/Papis M	6
		4	005	Pilot Racing	Ferte M/Campos A/Nearburg C	dnf
		-	011	Moretti Racing	-	dna

Other races

Date	Race venue	No	Chassis	Entrant	Drivers	Result
23.3.97	Monza	1	010	Moretti Racing	Moretti G/Montermini A/Hermann A	7
		2	012b	Horag Hotz	Lienhard F/Theys D	dnf

1998 – The USRRC Can-Am Series, a false dawn

The chaotic nature of the Professional Sports Car Racing organisation ensured that it would be shortlived. The owners of Daytona and Watkins Glen decided to cut loose from Evans at the end of 1997, and set up a championship with the co-operation of other smaller circuits that would run alongside the Professional Sports Car Racing series. The new organisation was entitled The United States Road Racing Championship, a name resurrected from the late 1950s. Its premier class was Can-Am (resurrected from the 1960s) and was run under the auspices of the Sports Car Club of America as a sanctioning body.

A combination of takeovers, splits and changes of title for the various factions did little to instil enthusiasm or confidence in the sports car scene. As a result, each organisation recorded losses, as competitors, sponsors, media coverage and spectators were even scarcer than during past seasons.

The 333 SPs built by Michelotto, in 1998, were easily distinguished from their predecessors. They had sleeker bodywork than previous models, with side radiators pushed back along the wings, and mounted at 45 degrees to the chassis. The 1998 versions would compete for both the USRRC, and the PSCR in America, and the ISRS Championship in Europe, alongside some of the older models, updated by the various teams that used them.

The Momo team, Bill Dollahite, and Doyle-Risi Racing, ran 333 SPs in both of the main series in America, while JB Racing, Autosport Racing SLR, and the Horag-Lista team drove the Ferraris in the ISRS in Europe. Scandia and Autosport Racing ran 333 SPs in the USAC, but not in the PSCR.

America

Daytona International Raceway, Daytona Beach, Florida, February 1

The highly-promoted opening race for the new USRRC series was held at Daytona. Scandia, Momo, and the new Doyle-Risi team each fielded a car. Enzo Calderari's Autosport Racing car failed to turn up. Ferrari 333 SPs dominated the qualifers.

Scandia opted for a high downforce setup to maximise speeds in and out of corners, while the Momo team, fielding its new car (#019), favoured a long-tailed body for top-end speeds on the straights. The Doyle-Risi team had no experience to draw on, and chose a compromise setup.

Weaver's Riley & Scott Mk III Ford took the lead, and held it, until it was involved in an accident, handing the top spot to the Doyle-Risi Ferrari.

During the late evening, van de Poele spun the Doyle-Risi Ferrari on some debris, and was pitched into the tyre wall at great force. His car had covered 225 laps.

The Scandia team was also encountering problems – a sticking throttle cost it time in the pits, followed by a much longer stop to cure a gearbox problem. The Ferrari returned to the track, only to have its engine die in a vivid display of smoke and flames.

At the front, the Momo Ferrari was chasing Rob Dyson's Riley & Scott Mk III Ford, and, after 21 hours of hard driving, the V-8 Ford engine lost power when two pistons collapsed. Baldi, driving the Momo Ferrari, seized his chance to take first place, and built up a considerable lead.

This gave him time to pit, and let Moretti take the wheel for the final 15 minutes. Moretti proudly took the chequered flag, achieving his dream of winning the Daytona 24-hour race.

Sebring International Raceway, Florida, March 23

The first round of the PSCR was a 12-hour race, held at Sebring International Raceway. Andy Evans had made the decision to withdraw his Scandia team permanently, which meant only two Ferraris were entered, the Daytona-winning Momo Ferrari, and that of the Doyle-Risi team.

Qualifying saw Wayne Taylor's Doyle-Risi Ferrari take pole, with the Momo Ferrari third. Didier Theys led the race, pulling some way ahead in the Momo Ferrari, helped by the demise of the two Riley & Scott cars directly behind him. The other Ferrari was plagued by fuel-system problems, which led to it retiring after 298 laps.

Despite a late charge by Andy Wallace, in a Panoz GTR-1, the Momo team hung on for a win, taking victory by one lap. In doing so, it accomplished a remarkable double in the Florida endurance races.

Las Vegas, Nevada, April 26

The first sprint race of the PSCR season provided a stark reality check for the race organisers. To put it simply, the event lacked both entrants and spectators. Only seven WSC cars turned up. Both the Momo and Dyson teams stayed away, weighing up their options.

The lone Ferrari there was a Doyle-Risi, driven by Wayne Taylor, who was given a stiff test by Murry's Riley & Scott, until the latter developed engine problems. Andy Wallace, in the Panoz GTR-1, took up the challenge, and the last 20 laps were nip-and-tuck, Taylor crossing the finish line a mere half-second ahead of the Panoz.

Homestead Speedway, Miami, Florida, May 17

The USRRC's response to the PSCR sprint race at Las Vegas was to stage a race at a new venue, Homestead Speedway.

Of the 27 entrants, 12 featured in the Can-Am class, with both the Momo and Dyson teams returning to the track, after their absence from Las Vegas. The other Ferrari present was the ex-Scandia 333 SP #004b, now campaigned by Bill Dollahite and Mike Davies.

Riley & Scott cars took the first row, with the Momo Ferrari third. The Dollahite Ferrari languished at the back, having had an engine change. For once, the Momo Ferrari was not consistently quick enough to challenge the Leitzinger/Weaver Riley & Scott. Baldi brought the 333 SP home in second place, just ahead of Wallace's Panoz. It was not an encouraging start for Bill Dollahite – his 333 SP retired after 81 laps, smoke pouring from its rear end.

Eric van de Poele

Eric van de Poele was born in Belgium in 1961. He was a former Formula One driver, participating in 29 GPs, debuting in March 1991. He later found considerable success in Touring cars before being signed up to drive sports cars. His first drive for the Doyle-Risi team in the WSCR Championship was at Sebring in 1998.

Eric van de Poele.
(Author's collection)

Lienhard and Theys drove their 333 SP to victory at Lime Rock. (Courtesy Andrew Hartwell)

Lime Rock, Connecticut, May 25

It was disappointing to see just nine WSC entries on the grid for the third round of the PSCR race series at Lime Rock, a low turnout not helped by three no-shows – one of them Bill Dollahite's Ferrari. He had failed to repair the previous week's damage at Homestead Speedway in time. The Doyle-Risi car was on the front row, alongside polesitter James Weaver's Riley & Scott, while the Lienhard/Theys car, entered by Kevin Doran, was down in seventh place.

Leitzinger, in a Riley & Scott, took the lead, a position that he never relinquished, while Taylor's Ferrari fought Forbes-Robinson for second spot. Pit stops shuffled the pack a little. Theys made up significant ground in the Doran Ferrari – so much so, that he was challenging the Leitzinger/Weaver car for the lead towards the end of the race. Theys

The Doyle-Risi entry driven by Taylor and van de Poele finished third at Lime Rock. (Courtesy Andrew Hartwell)

finished in a strong second position, just ahead of the Doyle-Risi Ferrari in third spot.

Mid-Ohio, Lexington, Ohio, June 14

Neither Momo, nor Doyle-Risi Ferrari attended the USRRC race at Mid-Ohio. Both teams had appeared at Le Mans a week earlier, and it would have been difficult to move cars and equipment back to America in time.

The only Ferrari to compete was Bill Dollahite's, and that made little contribution to the outcome of the race.

After qualifying tenth, the car failed to join the front runners, and, after numerous pit stops, could only manage 65 laps, finishing some 46 laps behind the winning car.

Road Atlanta, Braselton, Georgia, June 21

With Daytona and Watkins Glen now run by the USRRC, Road Atlanta was the second-longest race on the PSCR calendar after Sebring, running at ten hours or 1000 miles whichever came first.

Ferrari was represented by the Doyle-Risi team, and Kevin Doran's 333 SP #016. Both cars qualified well,

ending up on the first row of the 31-car grid, ahead of a pair of Riley & Scott Mk III Fords.

At the race start, Dorsey Schroeder's Riley & Scott squeezed between the two Ferraris to take the lead, and, within 30 minutes, Leitzinger had also passed the Ferraris.

An oil leak, and resultant fire, put the Theys/Lienhard Ferrari out of the race on lap 105, while the van de Poele/Taylor Ferrari finished in fourth place, after a couple of spins on the red Georgia clay surrounding the track.

Minneapolis, Minnesota, June 28

This new venue, for the USRRC, was a street circuit laid out in downtown Minneapolis. Only 18 cars took to the start grid. Of these, a mere six were in the Can-Am class.

It was becoming clear that the series was failing. The organisers had neglected to attract enough advertising, and had disastrously under-marketed the events. All the hype had been concentrated on the initial Daytona 24-hour race. Furthermore, the organisers had published grossly-inflated entry lists to attract spectators, but this short-term ploy was soon exposed, and the spectators, like the entrants, stayed away.

The Dollahite car #004b approaches the start grid at Mid-Ohio during practice. (Courtesy Tom Schultz)

The Doyle-Risi Racing entry #017 finished fourth in the race at Road Atlanta. (Courtesy Andrew Hartwell)

The only 333 SP present, #004b, the Dollahite/Davies entry, qualified third among the Can-Am cars, and finished seventh overall, four laps down on the winning Riley & Scott Mk III Ford driven by Weaver and Leitzinger.

Mosport Speedway, Bowmanville, Ontario, August 9

By August, the situation for the PSCR grid line-up was as desperate as that of the USRRC had been at Minneapolis. A total field of 15 cars, six of which were WSC cars, was all that could be mustered for the race at Mosport. Of those, two were the Ferrari of the Doyle-Risi team, and that of Kevin Doran.

Theys, in the Kevin Doran entry, took pole, while Taylor's car was fourth, and, for the first half-hour, it remained that way. Then both Ferraris rapidly fell back down the field. An electrical fault made Theys' engine misfire, and lose power, while Taylor had selected the wrong tyres, and struggled to maintain grip. The 333 SPs' problems were good news for the Panoz team – two of its cars moved ahead of the Ferraris. Theys finished in fifth place, followed by Taylor in the other Ferrari, two laps down on the race-winning Riley & Scott Mk III Ford.

Watkins Glen Raceway, New York State, August 23

A return to one of the spiritual homes of motor racing in America helped re-kindle the enthusiasm of entrants and spectators alike for the USRRC series. There were a respectable 31 starters for the six-hour race, with 12 Can-Am cars among their ranks. The USRRC organisers were determined to end their season with a flourish.

It was a special occasion for the Momo team too, as Gianpiero Moretti had announced that it would be the final race of his career. To mark this, the team gave him the honour of starting, before passing the driving duties to Theys and Baldi. The other 333 SP, #012b, was Bill Dollahite's. It was performing better than it had all season – until it took a spin, to finish only tenth.

Moretti started in third, but, with little time for sentiment among the drivers in a championship race, he was pushed further down the running order, and it was only when Theys took the wheel that things began to happen, as he clawed his way back through a throng of cars. By the time Baldi took over, he was only one lap adrift of Leitzinger in the leading Riley & Scott. An early tactical pit stop, under the pace car, allowed the 333 SP to gain more ground, until the car, now with Theys driving again, was just behind Leitzinger. When Leitzinger had to pit, it cost him the race. Theys crossed the finish line, winning Moretti a memorable retirement gift, as the Momo team took the third major American race of the season.

Sebring International Speedway, Florida, September 20

It was not a happy return to Sebring for the Doyle-Risi team. After taking pole for the three-hour race, ahead of Rob Dyson's Riley & Scott, the lone Ferrari entry managed only 11 laps before crashing out. Heavy rain had resulted in a red flag situation. When, after more than an hour's delay, the race was restarted, there were still puddles of water on parts of the track. Taylor inadvertently found one, spun, and scattered the tyre wall. That was the end of the race for the Ferrari.

Road Atlanta, Braselton, Georgia, October 25

Road Atlanta owner, Don Panoz, had already announced that, in 1999, he would back the new American Le Mans (ALMS) series. This year, the Petit Le Mans, a heavily promoted event held at Road Atlanta, would be a pilot event for it. The car classification for this race was more complex than usual, as both PSCR and ACO classes were eligible to compete. 31 cars qualified for the 1000km race, among them three Ferrari 333 SPs.

Kevin Doran's 333 SP started on the front row, the Doyle-Risi entry was fourth, and Bill Dollahite's car fifth. The Doyle-Risi car, #018, was the one used by the team at

Bill Dollahite's entry claimed fifth place at the Petit Le Mans, held at Road Atlanta. (Courtesy Andrew Hartwell)

Lazzaro, Davies and Dollahite shared the driving at the Petit Le Mans race. (Courtesy Andrew Hartwell)

After starting on the first row of the grid, the Theys and Lienhard car developed an oil leak, and a resultant fire ended its race at Road Atlanta. (Courtesy Andrew Hartwell)

Le Mans earlier in the year, and it ran in the LMP1 class, whereas the other two Ferraris ran in the WSC class.

The Doran Ferrari did not last beyond lap 59 – it developed a bad misfire, and Theys was forced to retire, to avoid more damage to the engine.

Meanwhile, the Dollahite Ferrari consistently ran in the top six, and finished a creditable fifth, covering 365 laps. It was left to the Doyle-Risi entry to uphold the honours for Ferrari. For much of the race, it was running second, behind Wallace's Panoz. Then the Panoz began to smoke, and came to a halt, leaving Taylor to lead for the remainder of the race, and take the chequered flag.

His victory set up a head-to-head fight between Taylor and points-leader Leitzinger, at Laguna Seca, for the Drivers' Championship title.

Bill Dollahite's entry finished fifth at the Petit Le Mans, held at Road Atlanta. (Courtesy Andrew Hartwell)

Laguna Seca, Monterey, California, October 25

The three regular Ferraris were entered for the final PSCR event of the season, the Doyle-Risi team reverting to its usual car (#017), though LMP1 cars were eligible for this event.

Uncharacteristically-poor weather prevailed for the whole weekend – after a heavy downpour of rain, the area was enveloped in a thick blanket of sea mist coming off the Pacific Ocean.

The wet conditions did not suit the Ferraris. Theys' car suffered from poor traction, and was then hit by a wayward BMW. It sent the Ferrari into a spin, costing time and its position in the tight field.

Taylor and van de Poele could only manage to finish sixth between them, in the highest-placed Ferrari. Theys and Lienhard were eighth, and Dullahite and Davies finished down in 13th place – a disappointing end to the season for Ferrari, after its successes at the major tracks in America.

Autosport Racing entry #020 seen at Monza, where it finished in second place in the hands of Calderari, Drynor and Angelo Zadra. (Courtesy Peter Collins)

Europe

Nine different Ferrari 333 SPs took part in the European and South African races, six of which were new-generation Michelotto cars.

Three of the 333 SPs ran at most of the events entered by JB Racing, Horag-Lista, and Autosport Racing SLR. GTC Motorsport attended two races, while later in the season GLV Brums participated in four races. The Moretti team and Doyle-Risi also made cameo appearances.

Monza, March 29

The Monza 1000km race was the first European race for the 333 SPs, a Euroseries GTR event. Three 333 SPs participated, Baldi taking pole, Taylor's 333 SP alongside him, and Calderari in fifth. It ended with newcomer Autosport Racing SLR the highest-placed – its Ferrari, driven by Calderari and Bryner, finished second, 11 laps behind the winning McLaren F1 GTR. The Doyle-Risi car was sixth, while the Moretti/Baldi 'European car' (#019) retired during a pit stop with a broken starter, having covered 132 laps.

Paul Ricard, April 13

Two weeks later, the first round of the ISRS series was held at the Paul Ricard circuit. Four 333 SPs were in the starting line-up of 15, and, for the first hour, were running 1-2-3-4, led by Collard in the JB Racing entry (#022).

Collard's hopes of a win were dashed, however, when a wheel-bearing seized, putting the car out of the race. Bellm's car #021 also went out, with a broken gearbox. The Theys/Lienhard car now inherited the lead, one that stretched all the way to the chequered flag. The remaining Ferrari, Calderari's, finished fifth.

Brno, May 17

The second round of the ISRS series was held at Brno. The same four 333 SPs were in attendance. This time Collard made up for the disappointment of the Paul Ricard event – leading the race throughout to take a well-deserved victory. Ray Bellm was also happier, finishing third, ahead

Lilian Bryner

Lilian Bryner was born in Switzerland in 1959. Lilian raced in the 1998 ISRS season with Autosport Racing until 1999, where she took two podium finishes before joining BMS Scuderia Italia for the 2001 FIA Sportscar championship series.

Lilian Bryner.
(Author's collection)

Taylor, van de Poele and Velez finished a creditable eighth in the Le Mans 24-hour race. (Courtesy Keith Bluemel)

of the older Theys/Lienhard car, and Calderari's car down in eighth.

Misano, May 23

A lone Ferrari, entered by Autosport Racing, turned up for the Misano six-hour race – another round of the Euroseries GTR, this one held at night under floodlights. Calderari's effort did not last very long: an oil pump seal failed, and the car retired after just 26 laps.

Le Mans, June 7-8

Eight 333 SPs were in the original entry list for the Le Mans 24-hour race, though only four turned up: those of JB Racing, Moretti Racing, Pilot Racing, and Doyle-Risi. Each car was prepared differently, the JB Racing entry, for instance, sporting 'long tail' bodywork, while the Michel Ferte car still had steel brakes and a five-speed gearbox.

Statistically, it looked unlikely that any of the Ferraris could mount much of a challenge – the original design was now five years old; ancient in terms of racing-car technology. Add to that the need to stop every nine or ten laps for fuel, and the odds were against them.

However, the Doyle-Risi team managed to finish the race in eighth place, having covered 333 laps – first in the LMP1 class, while the Moretti car was 13th overall, and third in the LMP1 class, despite an extended stop to repair the gearbox. The JB Racing 333 SP retired on lap 187 with a broken gearbox, and the Pilot Racing entry retired with a broken transmission shaft.

The JB Racing 333 SP passes the grandstands at Le Mans. (Courtesy Keith Bluemel)

The Pilot Racing 333 SP seen before the start of the 24-hour race at Le Mans. (Courtesy Keith Bluemel)

Misano, July 4

Ferrari's return to Misano for the ISRS night race turned out to be more productive than the previous visit by Autosport Racing in May. This time, three 333 SPs were on the start grid, with Calderari qualifying highest of the three, in fourth place.

After four laps, the JB Racing 333 SP was in the lead, and it never looked like being caught. With the Philippe Gache/Antony Beltoise Riley & Scott Mk III Ford securely in second place, the real race was for third. The two other Ferraris battled it out, and in the end it went to the Horag-Lista car, finishing just ahead of Calderari.

JB Racing's car #022 incorporated a 'long-tail' body for the race at Le Mans. (Courtesy Paul Kooyman)

Donington Park, July 19

The next stop on this European tour took the cars to Donington Park. There were fewer entrants than at Misano, with the usual three Ferraris the class of the field, topping the qualifying charts. Once more, the JB Racing 333 SP proved to be the pick of the bunch, taking an instant lead and gaining a substantial margin on the other two Ferraris, which were battling for second and third. In the final laps, the positions were consolidated as the Theys/Lienhard car pulled away from Calderari's 333 SP. A 1-2-3 was good news for Ferrari, no matter what order.

Anderstorp, August 16

Round five of the ISRS was held at Anderstorp. Heavy rain affected qualifying, but the conditions did not stop newcomer Giovanni Lavaggi from putting his recently-purchased ex-Scandia 333 SP (#003) fifth on the grid.

From the off, Collard's JB Racing Ferrari passed polesitter, Soper's Riley & Scott, and disappeared into the distance. The only time the other drivers saw the car again, was when it passed them. The fight was on between the Riley & Scott and the Theys/Lienhard 333 SP for second. It took until the final 30 minutes for Theys to make his passing move, to take second spot. Lavaggi drove cautiously to finish fourth, ahead of Calderari's car.

Nürburgring, September 6

The sixth round of the ISRS, at Nürburgring, was more challenging to the Ferraris than any previous round. The damp track proved to be the undoing of more than one car – it took just one lap to catch out Lavaggi, spinning and depositing his 333 SP into a gravel trap. Theys went ahead, while Collard, for JB Racing, made his way up through the field, after starting ninth. On the tenth lap, as the track began to dry, Collard took the lead.

Bad timing on a tyre change cost the Theys/Lienhard car dearly, and put them out of the running. To add to their woes, the car developed gearbox problems and had to retire. The Autosport Racing 333 SP also retired, after

Emmanuel Collard, in the driver's seat of #022, waits to leave the pit area at Donington. (Courtesy Keith Bluemel)

spinning and ending up in the track surrounds. This left the JB Racing entry to salvage something for Ferrari.

This it did, holding the lead to cross the finish line first, nine seconds ahead of Soper's Riley & Scott Mk III BMW.

Le Mans, September 19

Le Mans was the venue for the seventh round of the ISRS, a two-and-half-hour night race. Four Ferraris sat on the grid, the JB Racing entry on pole, with Martini's Riley & Scott Mk III BMW next to him, and Lienhard and Lavaggi on the second row.

Sospiri took the JB Racing 333 SP into an immediate lead, successfully negotiating an oil slick left by a BMW engine exploding shortly after the race start. Others were not so lucky. Theys spun and dropped back to 19th. Barring misfortune, the race was virtually won already, so great was Sospiri's lead. Theys made a valiant comeback to take second place, while Lavaggi finished fifth, and Calderari seventh.

Sospiri's three-lap victory-margin secured an ISRS win for the Ferrari 333 SP, the JB Racing team, and for Vincenzo Sospiri and Emmanuel Collard. As the Theys/Lienhard

Ferrari had also won the first round at the Paul Ricard circuit, it was a clean sweep for Ferrari on European soil.

Vallelunga, November 15

The Autosport Racing 333 SP #020 made one final appearance, at the Vallelunga six-hour race, held in November. Calderari claimed pole, and, after a strong race driven by Calderari, Bryner and Zadra, the car finished second, one lap down on the winner, the Tampolli RTA-Alfa Romeo.

South Africa

Kyalami, December 6

The final race of the ISRS was at the Kyalami circuit, in South Africa. To bolster the field, there were three cars over from America, including the Doyle-Risi 333 SP #017, driven by South African, Wayne Taylor.

Progress was much the same as it had been in Europe, with the JB Racing entry leading, well into the second half of the race, followed by a mix of Riley & Scott cars and Taylor's Ferrari. However, after the leading Ferrari pitted for a routine fuel stop, the starter motor failed to engage. Despite the efforts of the mechanics, the team were forced to retire the car. The Policand/Formato Riley & Scott Mk III Ford took the lead, and went on to win the race, spoiling Ferrari's 100 per cent record of victories in the ISRS.

Taylor/van de Poele finished third in the Doyle-Risi 333 SP, with Lavaggi fifth. The Theys/Lienhard Ferrari had disappeared from the lap charts early on, after a broken driveshaft ended their season prematurely.

Activity in the pit area captured during the practice session at Donington.
(Courtesy Keith Bluemel)

Sospiri and Collard drove #022 to victory at Donington. (Courtesy Keith Bluemel)

The Horag-Hotz 333 SP driven by Theys and Lienhard finished in second place at Donington. (Courtesy Keith Bluemel)

Professional Sports Car Racing World Sports Car Championship

Date	Race venue	No	Chassis	Entrant	Drivers	Result
22.3.98	Sebring 12hr	30	019	Momo/Doran	Theys D/Moretti G/Baldi M	1
		7	017	Doyle-Risi	Taylor W/van de Poele E/Velez F	6
26.4.98	Las Vegas	7	017	Doyle-Risi	Taylor W/van de Poele E	1
25.5.98	Lime Rock	27	016	Doran	Lienhard F/Theys D	2
		7	017	Doyle-Risi	Taylor W/van de Poele E	3
		88	004b	Dollahite	Dollahite W/Davies M	dna
21.7.98	Road Atlanta	7	017	Doyle-Risi	van de Poele E/Taylor W	4
		27	016	Doran	Theys D/Lienhard F	16
9.8.98	Mosport	27	016	Doran	Theys D/Lienhard F	5
		7	017	Doyle-Risi	Taylor W/van de Poele E	6
20.9.98	Sebring	7	017	Doyle-Risi	Taylor W	20
10.10.98	Road Atlanta	7	017	Doyle-Risi	van de Poele E/Taylor W/Collard E	1
		88	004b	Dollahite	Lazzaro A/Davies M/Dollahite W	5
		27	016	Doran	Theys D	dnf
25.10.98	Laguna Seca	7	017	Doyle-Risi	van de Poele E/Taylor W	6
		27	016	Doran	Theys D/Lienhard F	8
		88	004b	Dollahite	Davies M/Dollahite W	13

United States Road Racing Championship Can-Am Series (SCCA)

Date	Race venue	No	Chassis	Entrant	Drivers	Result
1.2.98	Daytona 24hr	30	019	Doran/Moretti	Moretti G/Luyendyk A/Baldi M/Theys D	1
		3	004b	Scandia	Dalmas Y/Wollek R/Papis M/Fellows R	20
		17	017	Doyle-Risi	Taylor W/van de Poele E/Velez F	dnf
		15	020	Auto Sport Racing	Bryner L/Calderari E	dna
17.5.98	Homestead	30	010	Moretti/Doran	Moretti G/Baldi M	2
		88	004b	Dollahite/Davies	Dollahite W/Davies M	12
14.6.98	Mid-Ohio	88	004b	Dollahite	Davies M/Dollahite W	dnf
		30	016	Doran/Moretti	Moretti G/Theys D	dna
28.6.98	Minneapolis	88	004b	Dollahite/Davies	Davies M/Dollahite W	7
23.8.98	Watkins Glen	30	016	Doran/Moretti	Moretti G/Baldi M/Theys D	1
		88	012h	Dollahite	Davies M/Dollahite W/Bourbonnais C	10

International Sports Racing World Cup Series

Date	Race venue	No	Chassis	Entrant	Drivers	Result
13.4.98	Paul Ricard	27	012b	Horag-Lista	Theys D/Lienhard F	1
		6	020	Autosport Racing	Bryner L/Calderari E/Zadra A	5
		2	021	GTC-Lanzante	Bellm R/Graf K	dnf
		5	022	Jabouille Bourresche	Sospiri V/Collard E	dnf
17.5.98	Brno	5	022	JB-Giesse	Sospiri V/Collard E	1
		2	021	GTC-Lanzante	Bellm R/Graf K	3
		27	012b	Horag-Lista	Theys D/Lienhard F	5
		6	020	Autosport Racing	Bryner L/Calderari E/Zadra A	8
23.5 98	Misano	1	020	Autosport Racing	Bryner L/Calderari E/Zadra A	dnf
4.7.98	Misano	5	022	JB-Giesse	Sospiri V/Collard E	1
		27	012b	Horag-Lista	Theys D/Lienhard F	3
		6	020	Autosport Racing	Bryner L/Calderari E/Zadra A	4
		17	023	Del Bello	Fabre P	dna
19.7.98	Donington	5	022	JB-Giesse	Sospiri V/Collard E	1
		27	012b	Horag-Lista	Theys D/Lienhard F	2
		6	020	Autosport Racing	Bryner L/Calderari E/Zadra A	3
16.8.98	Anderstorp	5	022	JB-Giesse	Sospiri V/Collard E	1
		27	012b	Horag-Lista	Theys D/Lienhard F	2
		12	003	GLV Brums	Lavaggi G/Bertaggia E	4
		6	020	Autosport Racing	Bryner L/Calderari E/Zadra A	5
6.9.98	Nürburgring	5	022	JB-Giesse	Sospiri V/Collard E	1
		6	020	Autosport Racing	Bryner L/Calderari E/Zadra A	dnf
		12	003	GLV Brums	Lavaggi G/Bertaggia E	dnf
		27	012b	Horag-Lista	Theys D/Lienhard F	Dnf
19.9.98	Le Mans	5	022	JB-Giesse	Sospiri V/Collard E	1
		27	012b	Horag-Lista	Theys D/Lienhard F	2
		12	003	GLV Brums	Lavaggi G/Thyrring T	5
		6	020	Autosport Racing	Bryner L/Calderari E/Zadra A	7
6.12.98	Kyalami	60	017	Doyle-Risi	Taylor W/van de Poele E	3
		12	003	GLV Brums	Lavaggi G/Chiesa A	5
		5	022	JB-Giesse	Sospiri V/Baldi M/Collard E	dnf

Date	Race venue	No	Chassis	Entrant	Drivers	Result
		27	012b	Horag-Lista	Theys D/Lienhard F	dnf
		6	020	Autosport Racing	Bryner L/Calderari E/Zadra A	dna

Le Mans

Date	Race venue	No	Chassis	Entrant	Drivers	Result
7.6.98	Le Mans 24hr	12	018	Doyle-Risi	Taylor W/van de Poele E/Velez F	8
		3	004b	Moretti Racing	Baldi M/Moretti G/Theys D	14
		5	022	Jabouille Bouresche	Boullion J/Sospiri V/Policand J	dnf
		10	005	Pilot Racing	Ferte M/Fabre P/Migault F	dnf
		9		Pilot Racing	Ferte M/Bell D	dna
		11	020	Ecurie Biennoise	Bryner L/Calderari E	dna
		6	021	GTC-Lanzante	Bellm R	dna
		4		La Filiere	Giraudi G	dna

Other races

Date	Race venue	No	Chassis	Entrant	Drivers	Result
29.3.98	Monza	3	020	Autosport Racing	Bryner L/Calderari E/Zadra A	2
		7	018	Doyle-Risi	Taylor W/van de Poele E	6
		30	019	Moretti Racing	Moretti G/Baldi M/Theys D	dnf
15.11.98	Vallelunga	5	020	Autosport Racing	Bryner L/Calderari E/Zadra A	2

The Sospiri/Collard car #023
in Parc Ferme at Nürburgring.
(Courtesy Peter Grootswagers)

Visit Veloce on the web – www.veloce.co.uk
Details of all books in print • Special offers • New book news • Gift vouchers • Web forum • And much more ...

76

1999 – European success for the 333 SP

For 1999, the USRRC reached an agreement with the ISRS in Europe, meaning that the two series would share the same rules for prototypes.

Entries for the USRRC series were sparse, and the final two rounds of the five-race series ended up being cancelled. At the end of the season, the series was taken over by the new Grand American Road Racing Association (Grand-Am). Just to add to the confusion for participants and spectators alike, a new race series was promoted by Don Panoz, entitled American Le Mans Series (ALMS). It was in effect a new name for the PSCR. ALMS used the same rules as the Le Mans 24-hour race, hoping to entice European teams to join the series in America.

In the United States, the Ferrari 333 SP faced stiff competition from the newer chassis of Riley & Scott, Lola, and Panoz. Furthermore, the four-litre Ferrari engine still had air restrictors, hindering its performance. The Doyle-Risi team decided to run with its 1998 333 SPs, feeling it was not necessary to buy new ones, and instead fitting the Michelotto modifications to its existing cars (#017 and #018).

America

Daytona International Raceway, Daytona Beach, Florida, January 31

This was round one of the USRRC series for 1999. A large starting grid of 78 cars included 20 Can-Am class entries, five of which were Ferrari 333 SPs, and six Riley & Scott Mk III Fords.

The 333 SPs qualified in second, third, fourth, seventh and 12th places, but Weaver's Riley & Scott took pole, and led the rain-hit race for the first five hours.

Another of the Riley & Scott cars eventually won the event, but three Ferraris were in contention for most of the way.

The Doyle-Risi car could have won, if it hadn't been hampered by prolonged pit stops to replace brake discs that were causing significant front-end vibration. Allan

The Doran Ferrari 333 SP sits in the pits at Daytona in front of the Matthews entry. (Courtesy Tom Schultz)

Autosport Racing brought #020 to the Daytona 24-hour race, where it chalked up a fourth place finish. (Courtesy Tom Schultz)

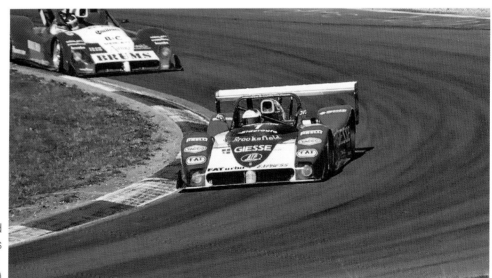

The Sospiri/Collard 333 SP #023 leads Lavaggi's car at Nürburgring (Courtesy Peter Grootswagers)

McNish did most of the driving in #018, and the team was rewarded with a second-place finish, one lap down on the winning Riley & Scott of Wallace, Forbes-Robinson and Leitzinger. Third, 14 laps behind, was the Doran-Matthews Racing Ferrari #026, followed by the Calderari/Bryner/Zadra 333 SP #020.

Defending champions, Theys, Baldi, Luyendyk and Lienhard, were among the first of the leading contenders to develop problems. Their car spent a long time in the pits with gearbox problems, falling back to 55th place, before eventually finishing eighth overall. The Dollahite Racing Ferrari, the oldest of the 333 SP chassis, #004b, qualified seventh, but went out with mechanical problems after 168 laps, the general consensus being that the car required better preparation to keep it competitive in its class.

Sebring International Raceway, Florida, March 20

The ALMS series started with the Sebring 12-hour race. It attracted 58 starters, 29 in the Prototype class.

Five 333 SPs were entered, but they were out-paced during qualifying, and started sixth, seventh, tenth and 25th. The new, more technically-advanced BMWs were first and third, separated by the Riley & Scott-Judd.

During the race, the highest place 333 SP, #018, was that of Taylor/Caffi/Fangio. It ran in second place for many hours, but eventually finished sixth, after a 40-minute pit stop to repair suspension damage caused when Caffi hit a retaining wall. The other four Ferraris failed to reach halfway – the two Dorans suffered gearbox failures, the Dollahite entry retired with an oil pump failure, and the second Doyle-Risi car suffered electrical failure.

Road Atlanta, Braselton, Georgia, April 18

The second round of the Le Mans Series saw five Ferrari 333 SPs on the grid. The two quickest qualifiers, neither of them Ferraris, had been put to the back for rule violations during practice, which put Weaver's Riley & Scott on pole, followed by the 333 SPs of Angelelli/de Radgues, #017,

Theys/Baldi, #025 and Taylor/Caffi, #018. The other two Ferraris started eighth and 14th.

Eric van de Poele's Riley & Scott took the lead, and headed the field throughout the race. The Baldi/Theys 333 SP gave chase, but ended up conceding victory by a margin of 24 seconds. The Angelelli/de Radigues car finished fourth, Taylor/Caffi sixth, with Doran-Matthews Racing finishing down in seventh, and Dollahite Racing ninth.

Lime Rock, Connecticut, May 31

Lime Rock, scene of past Ferrari victories, was the venue for the second round of the USRRC series. Two 333 SPs turned up, driven respectively by Lienhard/Theys and Matthews/Baldi. They started third and fourth on the grid of 24 cars.

The Forbes-Robinson/Leitzinger/Dyson Riley & Scott was set to win, but Dyson elected to take the wheel for the final stint. Leinhard had collided with Forbes-Robinson at the start of the race, but Theys was now back in contention in the 333 SP. With six laps to go, Theys tripped over a back-marker and spun, but he recovered, and finally passed Dyson with two laps left, to claim the victory.

On the seventh lap Matthews, in the other 333 SP, #026, was involved in an accident, and retired.

Mid-Ohio, Lexington, Ohio, June 6

This was the third, and turned out to be the last, round of the USRRC series. Although both the Doran-Lista and Doran-Matthews cars were in the original entry list, neither turned up for the race. Tight race schedules, and varying car specification regulations discouraged teams from entering into more than one series of races. Consequently the USRRC abandoned its series through lack of entries.

Mosport, Bowmanville, Ontario, June 27

The biggest news story at the ALMS race at Mosport came after qualifying – BMW Motorsport pulled its cars from the race, as the team had grave concerns over safety standards at the track. While it was not alone in voicing its unease, no other team withdrew its cars.

Qualifying demonstrated that the 333 SPs were going to struggle for pace, the Theys/Lienhard car highest placed in tenth.

The two Panoz cars maintained their qualifying form, and finished ahead of two Riley & Scott cars. The Ferraris were relegated to the status of 'also ran,' with Angelelli finishing fifth, Taylor seventh, and Theys eighth. The Dollahite entry retired after 61 laps, when the car spun off into the surrounding vegetation, and snagged and buckled the under-tray. The Matthews car lasted only eight laps before retiring with throttle problems.

Sears Point, Somona, California, July 25

Sears Point was won by a BMW, with the lead Ferrari finishing three laps down on the winner. However, if the 333 SPs could not mount a challenge for the lead, despite the arrival of a development engine, the contest to be first Ferrari across the finish line went right to the wire. The Doran team came out on top, Johansson beating Theys by less than half a second. Taylor's car had been the quickest in the early stages of the race, but crashed into a retaining wall on lap 73.

Portland International Raceway, Fountain, Oregon, August 1

The story for the Ferraris did not improve at Portland. Johansson was the highest qualifier, in sixth, with the other four cars strung out down the grid. For the first half of the race, Angelelli's 333 SP #017 looked set for a top three finish, until it began to misfire after de Radigues took over, eventually winding up in ninth.

Tenth, 11th and 12th places were also taken by the Ferraris of Dollahite, Taylor and Johansson, while the last of the 333 SPs, driven by Theys and Lienhard, failed to finish due to an accident, although it was classified as 38th on distance covered.

Road Atlanta, Braselton, Georgia, September 18

This 1000km event was a true endurance race, and was to test the Ferraris to the limit and beyond.

Theys' 333 SP was the slowest of the four in practice, but was the only one to finish, albeit eighth, 25 laps down on the winning Panoz.

Caffi went out on lap 172 after crashing, Angelelli on lap 187 with electrical problems, and Johansson on lap 225 with gearbox failure.

Laguna Seca, Monterey, California, October 10

Forty-three cars in a rolling start at Laguna Seca was a spectacular sight, especially for Ferrari fans, as the 333 SPs were up near the front of the grid, behind the quicker BMW, Lola and Riley & Scott cars.

A much better showing by Ferrari saw Johansson/Matthews finish fourth, behind two BMWs, and a Panoz LMP Roadster, while Caffi's 333 SP #018 finished sixth. The only Ferrari retirement was Angelelli's, out with gearbox problems on lap 102.

One of the Doyle-Risi Ferrari 333 SPs sits in the paddock at Laguna Seca. (Courtesy Martin Spetz)

Las Vegas, Nevada, November 7

The eighth and final ALMS race was held under lights. Again, Johansson, driving the Doran-Matthews car, was the best of the Ferrari contingent, finishing fifth, two laps down on the winning BMW. The two Doyle-Risi Ferraris finished four laps down, in seventh, and eighth, while the Theys/Baldi car crashed out on lap 47.

The Doran-Lista car emerges from the corkscrew at Laguna Seca. (Courtesy Martin Spetz)

Season summary for America

It was the end of a season that had seen the 333 SP increasingly uncompetitive in the Prototype class in ALMS, and the now defunct USRRC, races. Its fortunes in Europe were markedly different.

The second Doyle-Risi car in the paddock at Laguna Seca. Caffi/Taylor finished sixth. (Courtesy Martin Spetz)

#026 was run by the Doran-Matthews team, finishing fourth. (Courtesy Martin Spetz)

Europe

Additional teams lined up for the 1999 Sport Racing World Cup Series, some fielding new 333 SPs built by Michelotto. It was not unusual to find six or seven Ferraris sitting on the grid, as, despite the age of the design, they were still proving to be very competitive against the opposition in Europe.

Barcelona, March 28

The first round of the ISRS took place in Barcelona, with seven Ferrari 333 SPs amongst the total entry of 20.

Qualifying saw five Ferraris make the fastest times, with the two JB-Giesse cars vying for pole. In the event, the Collard/Sospiri car took pole, with the Baldi/Redon car alongside. During the race, the Ferraris proved very reliable, taking the top six places. The unfortunate seventh, driven by Waaijenberg and van der Lof, retired with a loose wheel just half a lap from the chequered flag. The experienced Collard/Sospiri team cruised to an untroubled win ahead of Pescatori/Moncini, with the second JB-Giesse car of Baldi/Redon third, one lap behind the leaders.

Monza, April 11

A record entry of eight 333 SPs turned up at Monza, but they were all out-qualified by the new Lola B98/10-Judd, driven by Gounon, Bernard and Tinseau. At the start, Bernard opened up a 13-second lead, the two JB-Giesse Ferraris giving chase. The halfway mark saw a change of fortunes, with the Lola having to pit with suspension problems. It returned, and was closing on the two JB-Giesse cars on lap 74 when its gearbox exploded. This left Collard to lead home Baldi, Calderari and Waaijenberg for a Ferrari 1-2-3-4 finish.

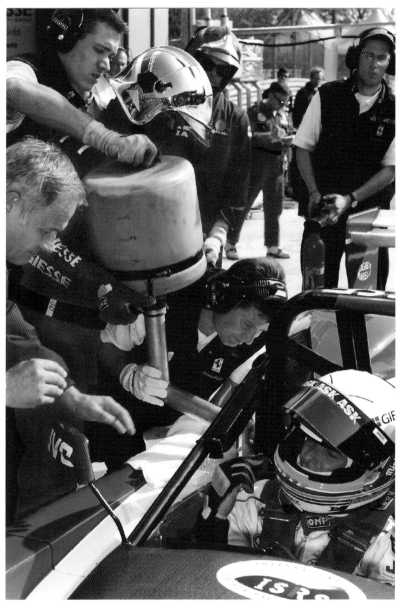

A routine pit stop for the JB-Giesse team at Monza. (Courtesy Helmut Schnug)

Driven by Sospiri and Collard for the JB-Giesse team, #023 showed its heels to the rest of the field, taking victory at Monza. (Courtesy Helmut Schnug)

Enzo Calderari captured in the 333 SP #020 at Monza. (Courtesy Helmut Schnug)

The Autosport Racing 333 SP finished a creditable third at Monza. (Courtesy Helmut Schnug)

The four other Ferraris failed to make it to the end of the race – Zadra/Zadra crashed #029 at Ascari curve on lap 28, Lavaggi retired on lap 39, while the other BMS Scuderia Italia pairing, Moncini/Pescatori, went out on lap 47. The American Doran-Lista car #016 had to retire on lap ten because of transmission problems.

Spa, May 16

Spa looked as though it would be a stiff test for the seven Ferraris entered, up against a surprise contender for honours – a Riley & Scott Mk III Judd. However, it was the Mauro Baldi/Laurent Redon 333 SP that won, beating its sister car, driven by Collard/Sospiri, the latter hit with a stop-go penalty for an indiscretion while following the safety car.

The two BMS Scuderia Italia cars finished fourth, and fifth, with Calderari in sixth place, two laps down on the winning car. The other two Ferraris retired, Lavaggi's car with a broken gearbox after 42 laps, and the Dutch National Racing team entry on lap 14, with similar gearbox problems.

The race-winning car at Spa driven by Baldi and Redon, closely followed by the Zadra father/son combination at Spa. (Courtesy Paul Kooyman)

Enzo Calderari and Lilian Bryner drove #020 to a sixth-place finish at Spa. (Courtesy Keith Bluemel)

Le Mans, June 13-14

There was to be no glorious return to Le Mans for Ferrari. Come the day, only one 333 SP – #030 driven by Baldi, Policand and Pescatori for JB-Giesse – was on the grid, down in 14th place. It was one of the chassis produced by Michelotto, #030, and was fitted with a new long-tail body. The Ferrari, started by Mauro Baldi, reappeared in the pits with gearbox problems just three laps after its first fuel stop. It was stationary for 75 minutes while the gearbox was changed, dropping from 26th to last place by the time it rejoined the race.

After slowly clawing its way up the leader board, the car was back in the pits on lap 71, the engine having lost power. A quick diagnosis confirmed damage had been caused by a broken cam cover, and that the problem was terminal.

Zadra/Zadra come out of the garage for practice on the Spa circuit. In the race they finished fifth. (Courtesy Peter Grootswagers)

#030 was driven by Baldi, Policand and Pescatori at Le Mans. (Courtesy Keith Bluemel)

JB-Giesse's #030 with a long-tail body at Le Mans. It retired with a broken cam cover. (Courtesy Paul Kooyman)

Pergusa, June 27

Just 16 cars made the trip to Sicily, but the small field included seven 333 SPs.

Larini's Riley & Scott qualified in pole, ahead of Pescatori, and, at the start of the race, both pulled away from the pack. It was not until the latter stages of the race that a quick pit stop by Pescatori gained him the lead, and he eased away to win by a margin of 64 seconds over Larini and Lorenzi. The JB-Giesse Ferraris suffered from a lack of pace, attributed to the effects of the 'success ballast' imposed on their cars. The new Ferrari of Giraudi/Tedeschi retired with gearbox failure, as did the Collard/Sospiri car.

Donington Park, July 18

Three weeks later, the cars were at Donington Park. The Lolas took first row, followed by Collard's and Lavaggi's Ferraris. Giraudi's 333 SP #031 had an accident in qualifying, and was too badly damaged to be ready for the race. The Lola B98/10-Judd took its first win, some 30 seconds ahead of Lavaggi's 333 SP #003. The GLV Brums car could have finished first, but it incurred damage in an incident with a back-marker, and was forced to make an extra pit stop. Collard led the race for a time, then an accident occurred so Collard took the opportunity to pit while the safety car was on track. However, on exiting the pits he failed to slot

The Autosport Racing 333 SP #020 could finish only eighth at Donington. (Courtesy Keith Bluemel)

Calderari's 333 SP #020 sits in the pit area
at Spa. The car finished sixth in the race.
(Courtesy Peter Grootswagers)

#029 on the start grid at Donington. It was driven by Marco and Angelo Zadra, finishing sixth. (Courtesy Peter Collins)

Lilian Bryner sits in the Ferrari 333 SP #020 at Donington. (Courtesy Peter Collins)

into his position behind the safety car and the mistake cost him dear.

All seven of the 333 SPs finished in the top ten cars.

Brno, August 1

The Brno race started with a bang – Pescatori spun the BMS Ferrari on the opening lap, and stopped broadside across the track. He was hit by Redon, who bounced off, and parked his 333 SP in the gravel. Pescatori managed to limp back to the pits with damaged rear suspension. After having the rear corner of the car changed, Pescatori returned to the race six laps down on his previous position.

Meanwhile, despite losing a wheel, the DAMS Lola-Judd raced to its second successive victory. It finished 58 seconds ahead of the JB-Giesse Ferrari driven by Collard and Sospiri. Collard was really going all out for the last ten laps, overtaking a Riley & Scott, and Angelo Zadra's Ferrari on the final lap.

Lavaggi retired with the starter motor jammed after covering 27 laps.

Nürburgring, September 5

The race at Nürburgring attracted 29 entries, with a record nine 333 SPs among them, including a rare appearance by the US-based Doran-Lista car, driven by Theys and Lienhard. Pescatori claimed pole, ahead of Bernard's Lola-Judd, but

#016 made a rare appearance in Europe, brought over to the Nürburgring from America by the Doran-Lista team. The car driven by Theys and Lienhard failed to finish. (Courtesy Keith Bluemel)

held the lead for just one lap, before Bernard overtook him. Pescatori, who drove for three sessions, remained close to the Lola-Judd, but never quite close enough to get ahead, finishing the race 15 seconds behind Bernard.

Third went to the Collard/Sospiri 333 SP #023, weighed down by 'success ballast.' It never threatened the leaders, but finished just ten seconds behind Pescatori's 333 SP. Most of the remaining Ferraris finished in procession 5th through to 9th, with only Lavaggi's, and Theys' cars failing to go the distance.

Magny-Cours, September 19

Lavaggi and Mazzacane took a maiden SRWC victory in the wet at Magny-Cours. Ferraris qualified for the first five places on the grid, with Pescatori taking pole. Terrible driving conditions, caused by heavy rain, took their toll, with three of the 333 SPs, driven by Collard, Baldi and Zadra, all leaving the track in separate incidents. It rained so heavily that the safety car was deployed on lap 37, and Pescatori cunningly used the safety period to complete two of his mandatory pit stops.

The result was only settled in the final few minutes, when the challenging Lola-Ford had to perform its final

Pescatori and Moncini drove #024 to second at the Nürburgring. (Courtesy Keith Bluemel)

pit stop, allowing Lavaggi to win by 18 seconds. Pescatori finished just over a minute behind, in third.

The results of the race left the Collard/Sospiri car just eight points ahead in the SRWC series, with one race to go.

Vallelunga, November 21

The six-hour race at Vallelunga, in November, was the seventh, and final, round of the GT Italian Challenge. A single 333 SP #031 turned up for the race, entered by Gianluca Giraudi, and was the only entry in the SR1 class. After taking pole in a field of 23, the car's performance mirrored the season that had now finished, only managing to finish in 15th, the last car running, due to an extended stop to replace a broken front hub. The car covered 198 laps, 50 laps down on the winning Tampolli RTA-98-Alfa, and, ironically, was first in class as it was running at the finish of the race.

South Africa

Kyalami, November 28

Ferrari drivers Collard and Sospiri won a second successive SRWC Drivers' Championship by the narrowest of margins at Kyalami, coming fourth behind race-winners Gounon and Bernard.

The race very nearly didn't happen. A tropical storm hit, causing chaos. Lightening sizzled around the Highveld, and the race was delayed for two hours. When it did start, it ran for just 90 minutes instead of the scheduled 180 minutes.

Zadra/Pescatori finished second, 17 seconds adrift of the Gounon/Bernard Lola-Ford, with Collard and Sospiri a further 20 seconds behind in fourth, just good enough to secure the Drivers' Championship, as well as the Teams' Championship? for their JB-Giesse team.

Professional Sports Car Racing World Sports Car Championship/ American Le Mans Series

Date	Race venue	No	Chassis	Entrant	Drivers	Result
20.3.99	Sebring 12hr	12	018	Doyle-Risi	Caffi A/Fangio J II/Taylor W/Angelelli M	6
		36	026	Doran	Kendall T/Matthews J/Dismore M	dnf
		27	025	Doran	Theys D/Baldi M/Lienhard F	dnf
		18	004b	Dollahite	Davies M/Dollahite W/Bundy D	dnf
		11	017	Doyle-Risi	Angelelli M	dnf
18.4.99	Road Atlanta	27	025	Doran	Baldi M/Theys D	2
		11	017	Doyle-Risi	Angelelli M/de Radigues	4
		12	018	Doyle-Risi	Caffi A/Taylor W	6
		36	026	Doran-Matthews	Kendall T/Matthews J	7
		18	004b	Dollahite	Davies M/Dollahite W	9
27.6.99	Mosport	11	017	Doyle-Risi	Angelelli M/de Radigues	5
		12	018	Doyle-Risi	Taylor W/Caffi A	7
		27	025	Doran-Lista	Theys D/Lienhard F	8
		18	004b	Dollahite	Davies M/Dollahite W	dnf
		36	026	Doran-Matthews	Lazzaro A	dnf

Date	Race venue	No	Chassis	Entrant	Drivers	Result
25.7.99	Sears Point	36	026	Doran-Matthews	Johansson S/Matthews W	8
		27	025	Doran-Lista	Theys D/Lienhard F	9
		11	017	Doyle-Risi	Angelelli M/de Radigues	10
		18	004b	Dollahite	Davies M/Dollahite W	14
		12	018	Doyle-Risi	Taylor W/Caffi A	dnf
1.8.99	Portland	11	017	Doyle-Risi	Angelelli M/de Radigues	9
		18	004b	Dollahite	Davies M/Dollahite W	10
		12	018	Doyle-Risi	Taylor W/Caffi A	11
		36	026	Doran-Matthews	Matthews J/Johansson S	12
		27	025	Doran-Lista	Theys D/Lienhard F	dnf
18.9.99	Road Atlanta	27	025	Doran-Lista	Theys D/Lienhard F/Dickens S	8
		36	026	Doran-Matthews	Johansson S/Matthews J/Dixon	dnf
		11	017	Doyle-Risi	Angelelli M/de Radigues/Pompidou X	dnf
		12	018	Doyle-Risi	Caffi A/Taylor W/Montermini A	dnf
		18	004b	Dollahite	Davies M/Dollahite W	dna
10.10.99	Laguna Seca	36	026	Doran-Matthews	Johansson S/Matthews J	4
		12	018	Doyle-Risi	Caffi A/Taylor W	6
		27	025	Doran-Lista	Theys D/Baldi M	13
		11	017	Doyle-Risi	Angelelli M/de Radigues	22
		18	004b	Dollahite	Davies M/Dollahite W	dna
7.11.99	Las Vegas	36	026	Doran-Matthews	Johansson S/Matthews J	5
		12	018	Doyle-Risi	Taylor W/Caffi A	7
		11	017	Doyle-Risi	Angelelli M/de Radigues	8
		27	025	Doran-Lista	Theys D	12
		18	004b	Dollahite	Davies M/Dollahite W	dna

United States Road Racing Championship Can-Am Series

Date	Race venue	No	Chassis	Entrant	Drivers	Result
31.1.99	Daytona 24hr	7	018	Doyle-Risi	McNish A/Taylor W/de Radiques/Angelelli M	2
		36	026	Matthews	Papis M/Johansson S/Vasser/Matthews J	3
		00	020	Autosport Racing	Calderari E/Zadra A/Bryner L Rosenblad C	4
		72	025	Doran	Theys D/Lienhard F/Luyendyk A/Baldi M	8

Date	Race venue	No	Chassis	Entrant	Drivers	Result
		88	004b	Dollahite	Davies M/Dollahite W/Bundy D/Dallenbach	dnf
31.5.99	Lime Rock	27	025	Doran-Lista	Lienhard F/Theys D	1
		36	026	Matthews	Matthews J	dnf
6.6.99	Mid-Ohio	27	025	Doran-Lista	Lienhard F/Theys D	dna
		36	026	Doran-Matthews	Matthews J	dna

International Sports Racing World Cup Series

Date	Race venue	No	Chassis	Entrant	Drivers	Result
28.3.99	Barcelona	1	023	JB-Giesse	Sospiri V/Collard E	1
		23	024	BMS	Moncini E/Pescatori C	2
		2	022	JB-Giesse	Baldi M/Redon L	3
		5	003	GLV Brums	Lavaggi G/Mazzacane G	4
		4	020	Autosport Racing	Bryner L/Calderari E	5
		22	029	BMS	Zadra M/Zadra A	6
		6	021	Dutch National	Waaijenberg D/van der Lof A	dnf
11.4.99	Monza	1	023	JB-Giesse	Sospiri V/Collard E	1
		2	022	JB-Giesse	Baldi M/Redon L	2
		4	020	Autosport Racing	Bryner L/Calderari E	3
		6	021	Dutch National	Waaijenberg D/van der Lof A	4
		5	003	GLV Brums	Lavaggi G/Mazzacane G	dnf
		22	029	BMS	Zadra M/Zadra A	dnf
		23	024	BMS	Pescatori C/Moncini E	dnf
		27	016	Doran-Lista	Theys D/Lienhard F	dnf
		26	031	Mastercar	Tedeschi F/Giraudi G	dna
16.5.99	Spa	2	022	JB-Giesse	Baldi M/Redon L	1
		1	023	JB-Giesse	Sospiri V/Collard E	2
		23	024	BMS	Pescatori C/Moncini E	4
		22	029	BMS	Zadra M/Zadra A	5
		4	020	Autosport Racing	Bryner L/Calderari E	6
		5	003	GLV Brums	Lavaggi G/Bscher	dnf
		6	021	Dutch National	Waaijenberg D/van der Lof A	dnf
27.6.99	Pergusa	23	024	BMS	Pescatori C/Moncini E	1
		2	022	JB-Giesse	Baldi M/Redon L	3

Date	Race venue	No	Chassis	Entrant	Drivers	Result
		22	029	BMS	Zadra M/Zadra A	4
		4	020	Autosport Racing	Bryner L/Calderari E	5
		5	003	GLV Brums	Lavaggi G/Mazzacane G	6
		1	023	JB-Giesse	Sospiri V/Collard E	dnf
		26	031	Kelemata	Giraudi G/Tedeschi F	dnf
18.7.99	Donington	5	003	GLV Brums	Lavaggi G/Mazzacane G	2
		1	023	JB-Giesse	Sospiri V/Collard E	3
		2	030	JB-Giesse	Baldi M/Redon L	4
		23	024	BMS	Pescatori C/Moncini E	5
		22	029	BMS	Zadra M/Zadra A	6
		4	020	Autosport Racing	Bryner L/Calderari E/Deletraz J	8
		6	021	Dutch National	Waaijenberg D/van der Lof A	9
		26	031	Kelemata	Giraudi G/Tedeschi F	dns
1.8.99	Brno	1	023	JB-Giesse	Sospiri V/Collard E	2
		22	029	BMS	Zadra M/Zadra A	3
		4	020	Autosport Racing	Bryner L/Calderari E	5
		23	024	BMS	Pescatori C/Moncini E	6
		2	030	JB-Giesse	Baldi M/Redon L	dnf
		5	003	GLV Brums	Lavaggi G/Mazzacane G	dnf
		26	031	Kelemata	Giraudi G/Tedeschi F	dna
5.9.99	Nurburgring	23	024	BMS	Pescatori C/Moncini E	2
		1	023	JB-Giesse	Sospiri V/Collard E	3
		2	030	JB-Giesse	Angelelli M/Baldi M	5
		22	029	BMS	Zadra M/Zadra A	6
		26	031	Kelemata	Giraudi G/Drudi L	7
		4	020	Autosport Racing	Bryner L/Calderari E/Deletraz J	8
		6	021	Dutch National	Waaijenberg D/van der Lof A	9
		5	003	GLV Brums	Lavaggi G/Mazzacane G	dnf
		27	016	Doran-Lista	Theys D/Lienhard F	dnf
19.9.99	Magny-Cours	5	003	GLV Brums	Lavaggi G/Mazzacane G	1
		23	024	BMS	Pescatori C/Moncini E	3
		1	023	JB-Giesse	Sospiri V/Collard E	dnf
		2	030	JB-Giesse	Baldi M/Policand J	dnf

Date	Race venue	No	Chassis	Entrant	Drivers	Result
		4	020	Autosport Racing	Bryner L/Calderari E/Deletraz J	dnf
		22	029	BMS	Zadra M/Zadra A	dnf
		6	021	Dutch National	Waaijenberg D/van der Lof A	dna
		26	031	Kelemata	Giraudi G/Tedeschi F/Drudi L	dna
28.11 99	Kyalami	22	029	BMS	Zadra A/Pescatori C	2
		1	023	JB-Giesse	Sospiri V/Collard E	4
		2	030	JB-Giesse	Baldi M/Policand J	5
		23	024	BMS	Pescatori C/Moncini E	6
		6	021	Dutch National	Waaijenberg D/van der Lof A	10
		5	003	GLV Brums	Lavaggi G	dna

Le Mans

Date	Race venue	No	Chassis	Entrant	Drivers	Result
13.6.99	Le Mans 24hr	29	030	Jabouille-Bouresche	Baldi M/Policand J/Pescatori C	dnf
		30	022	Jabouille-Bouresche	Baldi M/Policand J/Pescatori C	dnq
		-	005	Ferte	–	dna

Other races

Date	Race venue	No	Chassis	Entrant	Drivers	Result
7.11.99	Fuji	–		Pescarolo	–	dna
21.11.99	Vallelunga	7	031	Giraudi	Giraudi G/Drudi L/Parasitili R	15

Test day at Le Mans, #005 is wheeled along the pit lane during practice. (Courtesy Peter Grootswagers)

Visit Veloce on the web – www.velocc.co.uk
Details of all books in print • Special offers • New book news • Gift vouchers • Web forum • And much more ...

2000 – Introduction of the Grand-Am series

Founded in late 1999, the Grand American Road Racing Association was the successor to the defunct USRRC. It was centred around the Rolex 24-hour race at Daytona, but included a wide variety of American and Canadian tracks as well.

To the general public it was all very confusing. To fans who had supported the sport for years, one more name was hardly something to get enthusiastic about. Irrespective of the umbrella that covered them, the cars were the same, whether the series was called IMSA, Can-Am, PSCR, ALMS or Grand-Am.

In an attempt to give the 333 SP a new lease of life, the Doran-Lista team replaced the Ferrari V-12 engine with a Judd V-10 four-litre engine. It believed that, under the car-intake restrictor rules for ALMS, and the Sports Racing World Cup, the Judd engine would prove more competitive.

Of the Ferrari teams in America, only Doran-Lista and Risi entered races on a regular basis, with the Risi car running on a very limited budget.

Meanwhile, in Europe things were much brighter for the Sports Racing World Cup (SRWC). The series had become established the previous year, and there was still healthy support for it among the teams.

For 2000, there were to be two rounds of the Grand-Am – one at Daytona in June, the other at Road America in July. These would also count as rounds in the Sports Racing World Cup Series. However, the Grand-Am plans were later cancelled, due to the lack of willingness by European teams (other than JMB and BMS Scuderia Italia) to compete in America.

America

Daytona International Raceway, Daytona Beach, Florida, February 6

For this 24-hour race, there was a large field of 79 cars, 21 of which were from the SR1 class, including the Ferrari 333 SPs. The good news for Ferrari was that it qualified in second, sixth and 12th places – apart from that it was all bad news.

The Doran Ferrari, driven by Didier Theys, began well, setting the pace for the first part of the race, but almost from the start, the Risi Ferrari ran into problems. Caffi spun to the

The Risi team car #018 in the pit area at Daytona prior to the race. (Courtesy Tom Schultz)

back of the field on lap two, then, within the hour, there was a transmission issue – fitting a new gearbox was the time-consuming cure. It proved to be a temporary respite, however, as more gearbox problems put the car out on lap 162. Meanwhile, at the front, the battle raged between the Doran Ferrari and the Lola-Ford of Kenrod Motorsports. Around 6pm, the leading Ferrari slowed, with smoke coming from the engine bay. The 333 SP limped back to the pits, but the damage had been done, and the car was retired. "We had an air box fire. It has happened before at Portland in 1999. In a downshift deceleration mode, you get an over-run of fuel in the air box, and for some odd reason you get a backfire out of an air trumpet, and it ignites it, and all that excess fuel burns, and it takes out the injection wiring harness," explained a disappointed Kevin Doran.

The Autosport Racing entry with Calderai, Marco and Angelo Zadra and Bryner driving, fared little better, going out after 203 laps, also with the dreaded gearbox issues.

Theys, Baldi and Lienhard piloted #025 to a fifth place finish in the Sebring 12-hour race. (Courtesy Martin Spetz)

Sebring International Raceway, Florida, March 18

The 12-hour race at Sebring was the opening round of the 2000 American Le Mans Series (ALMS) season.

The only Ferrari to turn up was the Doran-Lista, with Theys, Baldi and Lienhard as drivers. A sign of the times was that Wayne Taylor and Eric van de Poele had joined the Cadillac team, taking with them Toshiba's sponsorship.

42 cars started, with the Ferrari 333 SP #025 ninth on the grid. Although never running in the top three, the car had a strong race, moving up the field to finish fifth, 23 laps down on the winning Audi R8, and 21 laps behind the fourth-placed car.

Domenico (Mimmo) Schiattarella

Domenico (Mimmo) Schiattarella was born in Italy in 1967. He drove in Formula One for Simtek in 1994, then in CART races before participating in the Grand-Am and ALMS races in America for the Risi team.

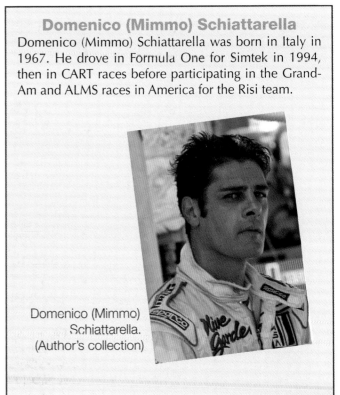

Domenico (Mimmo) Schiattarella. (Author's collection)

Phoenix International Raceway, Phoenix, Arizona, April 22

Twenty-three cars started this two-hour, 200-mile night race. The Doran-Lista, driven by Lienhard/Theys was third on the grid, while the Risi had teething problems, including the air box, and started a lowly 17th. New Risi team member Mimmo Schiattarella had best lap during qualifying cancelled due to an illegal air box, handing pole to Weaver.

The Weaver/Wallace Riley & Scott Mk III Ford dominated the first 48 laps of the race. Then Baldwin's Riley & Scott Mk III Judd took the lead. The two cars continued to swop the lead, but Kelleners/Schiattarella, in the Risi 333 SP #018, forced their way through the field to finish second, some 48 seconds behind Baldwin's winning car. The Doran-Lista was suffering the effects of an accident during practice, and finished fourth, two laps adrift.

Homestead Speedway, Miami, Florida, April 30

Twenty-nine cars lined up on the grid for the start of Homestead, with Baldi's 333 SP #025 on pole, and the Risi 333 SP in fifth.

Success for the Doran-Lista car came as a welcome surprise for the team, Baldi and Theys each taking a turn at the wheel. It finished ten seconds ahead of Jack Baldwin's Riley & Scott Mk III Judd, driven by Weaver/Paul, after a race-long battle, which only ended when the Riley & Scott succumbed to gearbox failure two laps from the finish.

The Risi entry ninth, eight laps adrift, after failing to show the pace it had at Phoenix one week earlier.

Lime Rock, Connecticut, May 29

Once again, the tight, twisty circuit at Lime Rock led to a small field, as the organisers restricted the eligible classes to SR1 and SR2.

The Risi 333 SP out-qualified the Doran-Lista entry, starting on the front row, alongside the Weaver/Leitzinger Riley & Scott Mk III Ford. Schiattarella's 333 SP and Weaver's

Riley & Scott clashed at the first corner, handing an early lead to Theys, driving the Doran-Lista. Weaver recovered to take the win, but Theys remained in second place, with the Risi, driven by Schiattarella/Kelleners third.

Mid-Ohio, Lexington, Ohio, June 4

A third 333 SP turned up for the Mid-Ohio race, entered by Brown Motorsports. The 333 SP #026 was previously owned by Doran Enterprises and Doran Matthews Racing. The car had been entered by Brown Motorsports for both Phoenix, and Homestead, but had failed to show at either event, so this was its maiden race under current ownership.

The Risi entry started fifth, but the troubled Doran-Lista car was 21st and Brown Motorsport 22nd. Theys/Baldi, driving the Doran-Lista, fought their way through the field, to finish a creditable fifth.

Daytona International Raceway, Daytona Beach, Florida, June 29

With a start time of 10pm, there were very few spectators to watch the race at Daytona. Out of a field of 42 cars, there were two Ferrari 333 SPs, the Doran-Lista #025, and the Risi #018. The Risi 333 SP took third position on the grid, while the Doran-Lista car was fifth.

Weaver's Riley & Scott took the lead, and held it for the initial eight laps, before being overtaken by Kelleners in the 333 SP. Kelleners lead was brief – first Weaver, and then Theys, passed him. They held their positions, Weaver winning by just four seconds. Towards the end, the Kelleners/Schiattarella 333 SP was closing on Theys, and only one second separated them as they crossed the finish line.

Road America, Elkhart Lake, Wisconsin, July 9

Among a field of 40 cars, the Doran-Lista 333 SP dominated, earning pole, ahead of the two Riley & Scott cars of Wallace and Baldwin, and the Risi on row two.

Kevin Doran's Ferrari 333 SP-Judd sits on the grid at Lime Rock, together with the team members.
(Courtesy Andrew Hartwell)

After trailing in the wake of Weaver's Riley & Scott for 20 laps, the Doran Lista car took the lead on lap 21 and held it for 30 laps, before giving way to the number 16 Riley & Scott once more.

On lap 105, as the cars pitted, the Risi Ferrari found its way to the front. However, it was passed by the Doran-Lista Ferrari, which went on to take victory, with the Risi just four seconds behind as the chequered flag fell.

Trois-Rivières, Quebec, July 30

Twenty-seven starters took to the grid, the Doran-Lista Ferrari #025 on pole, and the Risi 333 SP #018 in fourth spot.

Theys led the early laps, but his advantage was wiped out by a caution period. At the restart, the Ferrari was struggling for grip, and Weaver's Riley & Scott Mk III Ford surged ahead. Theys/Bentley drove the Doran-Lista car to finish in second place, four seconds behind the winning

The Risi entry was driven by Schiattarella and Kelleners, finishing third overall at Lime Rock. (Courtesy Andrew Hartwell)

#025 finished second at Lime Rock, driven by Theys and Lienhard. (Courtesy Andrew Hartwell)

Weaver/Leitzinger Riley & Scott. Kelleners/Schiattarella finished fifth in the other 333 SP, one lap down.

Watkins Glen International Raceway, New York State, August 17

For both Risi and Doran-Lista teams, the final race of the Grand-Am series was one to forget. This year, there had been a 100km race scheduled for Friday evening, but it was reduced to 50km due to rapidly fading light. Theys finished in second place while Schiatarella was fourth overall. These finishing positions were carried over as starting positions for the six-hour race

After setting competitive times for the six-hour race, to start second and fourth on the grid of 52, things went downhill for the Ferraris.

Theys, in the Doran-Lista Ferrari, started well, taking the lead from Weaver's Riley & Scott on the first corner. However, on the 85th lap, the Doran-Lista car sustained crash damage, and was forced to retire. The Risi 333 SP managed 118 laps, and was running in third place, when

333 SP number 27 (#025) and 333 SP number 12 (#018) line up for qualifying positions on the grid at Road America. (Courtesy Tom Schultz)

Mimmo Schiattarella driving #018 to a second place finish at Road America. (Courtesy Tom Schultz)

its air box caught fire, putting paid to any further progress. Weaver reclaimed the lead shortly before the race's end to take the win.

Europe

While the number of active 333 SPs had dwindled in America, the marque was still very active and competitive in Europe. Among the teams running Ferraris was the JMB team – formerly JB, before an amicable split between JM Bouresche and JP Jabouille.

Barcelona, March 26

The first round of the Sports Racing World Cup Series began in Barcelona. 18 cars took to the grid, five 333 SPs among them.

Lavaggi raised a few eyebrows by claiming pole in the GLV Brums Ferrari, while the other Ferraris occupied fourth, sixth, ninth and 11th places.

Collard's Cadillac Northstar leapt into an unexpected lead for a lap, while the Lavaggi and Pescatori Ferraris scrapped for second place. However, once past the Cadillac, the two Ferraris quickly broke away from the pack.

Terrien took over from Pescatori in the JMB Ferrari, and put in a measured drive to win by a comfortable margin of twenty seconds over the GLV Brums entry. The BMS Scuderia Italia team had a quiet weekend, Peter/Marco Zadra came through to finish fourth, just ahead of the team's second car driven by Bryner, Calderari and Angelo Zadra. The new Cauduro Tampolli team car #031 (the ex-Italtechnia car) finished ninth, seven laps down on the winning Ferrari

Monza, April 16

Three weeks later, the scene moved to Monza, where the Baldi/Formato Riley & Scott Mk III Judd saw off the Barcelona race winners, Pescatori and Terrien. The JMB Ferrari started in eighth place, after a troubled qualifying session. Six Ferraris were entered for this 'home fixture,' with the GLV Brums entry highest on the grid in third.

It was left to Pescatori/Terrien to fight for honours – the Peter/Marco Zadra BMS Scuderia Italia entry retired after 11 laps with engine failure, and the GLV Brums Ferrari's race ended two-thirds of the way through with a broken differential. The second BMS car finished fifth, three laps down, and the Dutch National Racing entry sixth, four laps down, while the Tampolli car was 11th, having had electrical problems throughout the race.

Spa, May 21

The infamous Ardennes weather upset the fortunes of many of the major SR1 class teams at Spa. Nobody could have predicted that a car from the SR2 class would win the race – but it did, with many of the SR1 cars hitting trouble, as lashing rain fell for most of the two and a half-hour race.

On the second lap, Marco Zadra, in the lead BMS Ferrari, spun out at the chicane, extensively damaging the rear wing, while the GLV Brums car exited the race on lap 13 with engine failure.

The Pescatori/Terrien Ferrari was up with the leading cars for much of the race, and, with the high attrition rate, it looked a likely candidate to win – only for the car to slow suddenly with an irreparable drivetrain problem. It was left to creep round the circuit and finish fifth.

The race went to the wire, however, with a Lucchini-Alfa 99 holding out for victory, just two seconds ahead of Angelo Zadra's BMS Ferrari. It could have been very different for the 333 SP, had the team not miscalculated the number of laps left to run. The team thought it were on the penultimate lap, and had plenty of time to pass the Lucchini, and was caught out when the chequered flag suddenly appeared.

Nürburgring, July 9

The July event at Nürburgring was part of the 2000 American Le Mans Series (ARMS). The 1000km race attracted a field of 38, with just the GLV Brums car #003 to represent Ferrari. Lavaggi started 13th. In torrential rain, he and Filiberti had a steady drive that took them up the field to finish seventh, having covered 177 laps – only eight laps behind the winning Panoz LMP-1 driven by Magnussen and Brabham.

It was no fun for Pescatori and Terrien driving in the rain at Spa.
(Courtesy Paul Kooyman)

Brno, August 6

A meagre field of 15 cars turned up at Brno, including five 333 SPs. Wet conditions at the start turned the race on its head for a while. Once the track dried, however, the Ferraris of Terrien, Lavaggi and Marco Zadra came to the fore.

After settling down on slick tyres for the latter half of the race, Pescatori/Terrien pulled out a 30-second lead over Baldi's Riley & Scott Mk III Judd to cruise home for the final 20 laps. Lavaggi finished two seconds behind Baldi, with Marco Zadra in fourth place, a further seven seconds adrift.

Enzo Calderari endured a torrid time, including five pit stops, but salvaged sixth place ahead of the Dutch National Racing Ferrari that had performed well in the first hour when conditions were wet.

All five of the 333 SPs finished in the top seven places.

Donington Park, August 27

Six 333 SPs were in attendance at Donington. A rolling-start lap incident at Donington Park put three main contenders out of the running immediately, giving the Ferrari runners a great chance of winning the race – the front half of the grid had accelerated out of the final corner of the rolling-lap, only to lift off when the drivers saw the red light was still on. In the confusion, Panoz driver John Neilsen shunted Baldi's Riley & Scott into the barriers putting both cars out of the race.

Pescatori/Terrien made the most of that opportunity, going on to win by over a lap, ahead of Marco Zadra and Enzo Calderari's 333 SPs to give Ferrari a 1-2-3 finish. The Tampolli Ferrari finished fifth, while Lavaggi was the driver to miss out – the GLV Brums car had gone into a spin and ended up deep in a gravel trap and out of the race, with co-driver Filiberti at the wheel.

Pescatori/Terrien's win opened their championship lead to 33 points, giving them an almost unassailable margin. Just one more victory would be enough to claim the title for the JMB team and the drivers.

David Terrien sits in #030 on the grid at Donington. (Courtesy Peter Collins)

The JMB-Giesse team car #030 was victorious at Donington. (Courtesy Peter Collins)

Philipp Peter and Marco Zadra claimed second place at Donington driving #024. (Courtesy Peter Collins)

Nürburgring, September 17

Twenty-three cars – the largest field of the season – lined up on the grid at Nürburgring for round six of the Sports Racing World Cup. Among them there were seven Ferraris, the largest number at any meeting held in Europe. The entry was bolstered by an eagerly-awaited addition to the European ranks, the American-based Doran Ferrari 333 SP-Judd, driven by Didier Theys and Fredy Lienhard.

Wet conditions were becoming a theme at the European races, and, again, it was Pescatori/Terrien who adapted quicker than others, taking the lead ten laps from the end and claiming the victory. This win gave the JMB team the Team Championship, and Pescatori and Terrien the Drivers' Championship.

The French JMB team not only completed a hat-trick of titles in the SRWC, but managed it in emphatic fashion. Marco Zadra brought the BMS Ferrari home in second place, while Filiberti/Lavaggi came fifth, their car having suffered tyre problems in the first half of the race. The second BMS car was seventh, followed by the Dutch National Racing entry in ninth. The Doran entry was not set up for wet conditions and struggled into 11th place, four laps down on the winner.

Magny-Cours, October 1

Title champions Pescatori and Terrien did not rest on their laurels. At the penultimate championship race at Magny-Cours, they pulled away from the rest to win by a margin of 40 seconds over Lavaggi's and Zadra's 333 SPs.

This was the second Ferrari 1-2-3 of the season, proving yet again that there was still life in this venerable car. Calderari, Bryner and Angelo Zadra hung on to their equal third place in the Drivers' Championship after finishing the race fifth.

With the top teams still keen to race the 12 cylinder engine for another season, it seemed incredible that Michelotto should wish to stop technical support. Michelotto considered that without a significant amount of money being spent on the development of the car (and Ferrari would not commit to that), it had gone as far as it could.

South Africa

Kyalami, November 26

A disappointingly small field of 12 cars turned up at Kyalami for the final round of the SRWC Championship.

Only three Ferraris attended, two from the BMS Scuderia Italia team, and one entered by the GLV Brums team. With the Championship already in the bag, the JMB team declined to take up its entry.

In its absence, the Lola-Ford of Formato/Kelleners built up a lead of 50 seconds and went on to take the win – they nearly lost it to Peter/Angelo Zadra in one of the BMS Ferraris, after a faulty fuel rig left the Lola-Ford under-fuelled. The team was powerless to help as Kelleners' 50-second lead evaporated, and he won the race by only four seconds, ahead of the BMS Ferrari. Lavaggi came third, some 38 seconds behind.

The second BMS Ferrari went out of the race suffering from a stuck throttle, after qualifying sixth on the grid, denying the drivers Calderari, Bryner and Angelo Zadra the chance to improve on third in the Drivers' Championship.

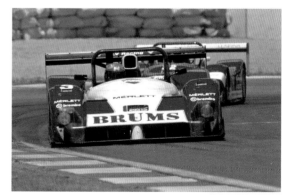

Lavaggi and Filiberti drove an old 333 SP #003 to a third place finish at Kyalami. (Courtesy Keith Bluemel)

Grand American Road Race Championship (Grand-AM)

Date	Race venue	No	Chassis	Entrant	Drivers	Result
6.2.00	Daytona 24hr	00	020	Autosport Racing	Calderari E/Zadra A/Zadra M/Bryner L/Rosenblad C	dnf
		12	018	Risi	Caffi A/McNish A/Kelleners R/Schiattarella R	dnf
		27	025	Doran Enterprises	Theys D/Lienhard F/Bentley R	dnf
		11	017	Risi	Caffi A/McNish A/Kelleners R/Schiattarella R	dna
22.4.00	Phoenix	12	018	Risi	Schiattarella R/Kelleners R	2
		27	025	Doran-Lista	Theys D/Lienhard F	4
		2	026	Brown Motorsports	–	dna
30.4.00	Homestead	27	025	Doran-Lista	Baldi M/Theys D	1
		12	018	Risi	Schiattarella R/Kelleners R	9
		2	026	Brown Motorsports	–	dna
29.5.00	Lime Rock	27	025	Doran-Lista	Theys D/Lienhard F	2
		12	018	Risi	Schiattarella R/Kelleners R	3
4.6.00	Mid-Ohio	12	018	Risi	Schiattarella R/Kelleners R	4
		27	025	Doran-Lista	Theys D/Baldi M	5
		2	026	Brown Motorstorts	Brown/Dickens S	27
29.6.00	Daytona	27	025	Doran-Lista	Theys D/Bentley R	2
		12	018	Risi	Schiattarella R/Kelleners R	3
		2	026	Brown Motorsports	Brown/Dickens S	dna
9.7.00	Road America	27	025	Doran-Lista	Theys D/Lienhard F/Baldi M	1
		12	018	Risi	Schiattarella R/van de Poele E	2
		2	026	Brown Motorsports	Brown/Dickens S	dna
30.7.00	Trois-Rivieres	27	025	Doran-Lista	Theys D/Bentley R	2
		12	018	Risi	Schiattarella R/Kelleners R	5
		2	026	Brown Motorsports	Brown/Dickens S	dna
16.8.00	Watkins Glen	27	025	Doran	Theys D	2
		12	018	Risi	Schiattarella R	4
17.8 00	Watkins Glen	12	018	Risi	Schiattarella R/Kelleners R/van de Poele E	dnf
		27	025	Doran-Lista	Theys D/Lienhard F/Bentley R	dnf

American Le Mans Series

Date	Race venue	No	Chassis	Entrant	Drivers	Result
18.3.00	Sebring 12hr	27	025	Doran-Lista	Theys D/Baldi M/Lienhard F	5

Sports Racing World Cup

Date	Race venue	No	Chassis	Entrant	Drivers	Result
26.3 00	Barcelona	1	030	JMB Giesse	Pescatori C/Terrien D	1
		3	003	GLV Brums	Lavaggi G/Fiilberti N	2
		23	024	BMS	Peter P/Zadra M	4
		22	029	BMS	Bryner L/Calderari E/Zadra A	5
		28	031	Tampolli	Giraudi G/Lancelotti A	9
		6	021	Dutch National	Waaijenberg D/van der Lof A	dnf
16.4.00	Monza	1	030	JMB Giesse	Pescatori C/Terrien D	2
		22	029	BMS	Bryner L/Calderari E/Zadra A	5
		6	021	Dutch National	Waaijenberg D/van der Lof A	6
		3	003	GLV Brums	Lavaggi G/Fililberti N	dnf
		23	024	BMS	Peter P/Zadra M	dnf
		28	031	Tampolli	Giraudi G/Lancelotti A	dnf
21.5.00	Spa	22	029	BMS	Bryner L/Calderari E/Zadra A	2
		1	030	JMB Giesse	Pescatori C/Terrien D	5
		3	003	GLV Brums	Lavaggi C/Filiberti N	dnf
		6	021	Dutch National	Waaijenberg D/van der Lof A	dnf
		23	024	BMS	Peter P/Zadra M	dnf
		28	031	Tampolli	Giraudi G	dna
9.7.00	Nurburgring	18	003	GLV Racing	Lavaggi C/Fiilberti N	7
6.8.00	Brno	1	030	JMB Giesse	Pescatori C/Terrien D	1
		3	003	GLV Brums	Lavaggi C/Fiilberti N	3
		23	024	BMS	Peter P/Zadra M	4
		22	029	BMS	Bryner L/Calderari E/Zadra A	6
		6	021	Dutch National	Waaijenberg D/van der Lof A	7
27.8.00	Donington	1	030	JMB Giesse	Pescatori C/Terrien D	1
		23	024	BMS	Peter P/Zadra M	2
		22	029	BMS	Bryner L/Calderari E/Zadra A	3
		28	031	Tampolli	Giraudi G/Burton J	5
		3	003	GLV Brums	Lavaggi C/Filiberti N	dnf
		6	021	Dutch National	Waaijenberg D/van der Lof A	dnf
17.9.00	Nurburgring	1	030	JMB Giesse	Pescatori C/Terrien D	1
		23	024	BMS	Peter P/Zadra M	2

Date	Race venue	No	Chassis	Entrant	Drivers	Result
		3	003	GLV Brums	Lavaggi G/Filiberti N	5
		22	029	BMS	Bryner L/Calderari E/Zadra A	7
		6	021	Dutch National	Waaijenberg D/van der Lof A	8
		28	031	Tampolli	Giraudi G/Parasitili R	9
		27	025	Doran-Lista	Theys D/Lienhard F	11
1.10.00	Magny-Cours	1	030	JMB Giesse	Pescatori C/Terrien D	1
		3	003	GLV Brums	Lavaggi G/Filiberti N	2
		23	024	BMS	Peter P/Zadra M	3
		22	029	BMS	Bryner L/Calderari E/Zadra A	5
		28	031	Tampolli	Giraudi G/Burton J	dnf
26.11.00	Kyalami	23	024	BMS	Peter P/Zadra M	2
		3	003	GLV Brums	Lavaggi G/Filiberti N	3
		22	029	BMS	Bryner L/Calderari E/Zadra A	dnf

Le Mans

Date	Race venue	No	Chassis	Entrant	Drivers	Result
18.6.00	Le Mans 24hr	18	018	Risi	Schiattarella M/Caffi A/Kelleners R	dna
			003	GLV Brums	Lavaggi G	dna
			005	BSM/Michel Ferte	Ferte M/Ferte/Fabre P	dna
				BMS	–	dna
				Jabouille-Bouresche	–	dna
				Jabouille-Bouresche	Pescatori C/Terrien D	dna

2001 – Winding down – the end of an era

America

Only two Ferrari 333 SPs were used in competition in America during 2001. Risi Competizione fielded #037 at the Daytona 24-hour race, while six other rounds of the Grand-Am Championship were attended by a Ferrari 333 SP-Judd, a Lista-Doran team, the same car as had campaigned in 2000, #025, entered under the name of Doran-Lista Racing.

No Ferrari 333 SPs were entered in the ALMS series.

Daytona International Raceway, Daytona Beach, Florida, February 4

The lone 333 SP entry at Daytona, the Risi Competizione #037, qualified third. As early as lap ten, with Ralf Kellners driving, it took the lead after a tense, but short, struggle with the Dyson Riley & Scott Mk III Ford. Then Allan McNish established a gap of twenty seconds for the Ferrari, extending it to a minute when Leitzinger pitted the Riley & Scott.

After three hours, it began to rain. The wet weather proved a major handicap for the Risi Ferrari. With just over 200 laps completed, it lost the lead due to an unscheduled stop to get the headlights working. 50 laps later, the 333 SP lost a wheel, which had not been re-fitted properly after a brake change, and McNish limped to the pits on three wheels. The Ferrari pushed on until the 16th hour, when it suffered engine failure and went out of the race, having covered 463 laps.

Some night-time action from the Daytona 24-hour race.
(Courtesy FOC Great Britain)

The Risi team Ferrari number 12 was classified 46th after delays hampered its progress throughout the race at Daytona. (Courtesy FOC Great Britain)

A night-time pit stop for the Risi team car #037 at Daytona. (Courtesy FOC Great Britain)

The Risi team car #037 went out of the Daytona 24-hour race after covering 463 laps. (Courtesy FOC Great Britain)

Watkins Glen International Raceway, New York State, May 19

Round four of the Grand-Am Championship saw the introduction of the Lista-Doran Ferrari 333 SP-Judd for its first race of the season. The car made an immediate impact, qualifying second of 37, alongside Wallace's Riley & Scott Mk III Ford. Theys, Baldi and Lienhard kept the Ferrari at the head of the pack, contending the lead with Weaver's Riley & Scott Mk III Ford. Then, during the final laps, the Riley & Scott dropped a cylinder, and the swept past to take the lead. After six gruelling hours, the Ferrari crossed the finish line to register a fine, if unexpected, victory.

Lime Rock, Connecticut, May 28

Buoyed by their success at Watkins Glen, the Lista-Doran team turned up at Lime Rock for round five of the Grand-Am Championship, a two-heat sprint over the scenic, but twisty, narrow circuit. The first sprint was 40 minutes long; the second 45, with the grid for the second sprint based on the results of the first. Only ten cars made it to the grid: an even lower than usual number for this venue.

With Theys driving, the 333 SP sustained some damage in practice, but Baldi and Theys still managed to qualify third for both heats, and, indeed, finished third in both races.

Mid-Ohio, Lexington, Ohio, June 10

Forty-one cars lined up for the 250-mile race at Mid-Ohio, with the Baldi/Theys Ferrari 333 SP-Judd on the second row.

The lead was fiercely contested between the Lola-Judd driven by Oliver Gavin, and James Weaver's Riley & Scott, while the Ferrari finished third, one lap down.

Road America, Elkhart Lake, Wisconsin, July 7

The 500-mile race at Road America attracted a field of 37, with Lienhard joining Theys and Baldi for this longer-distance race.

Theys started on the front row, and, early on, was left unchallenged for a time when fellow-pacemaker James Weaver developed engine problems, and was forced to retire. Elliott Forbes-Robinson took up the challenge, overtaking the Ferrari and going a lap clear, only to lose his advantage when the yellow flags were raised and the Ferrari closed the gap. With nine laps remaining, Theys regained the lead to win by the very narrow margin of 1.6 seconds over the Forbes-Robinson/Schroeder Riley & Scott Mk III Judd.

Trois-Rivières, August 5

Only 15 starters appeared on the grid for the eighth round of the Grand-Am Championship, a 92-lap race at Trois-Rivières. This was partly because an ALMS race had taken place at Portland on the same day. The Lista-Doran 333 SP-Judd qualified fifth, but never challenged the lead cars. Bentley co-drove the 333 SP with Theys, and had a close race for third place with Forbes-Robinson in the Riley & Scott Mk III Judd, with the Ferrari finishing third, 17 seconds down on the winning Riley & Scott Mk III Ford, driven by Weaver and Leitzinger.

Watkins Glen International Raceway, New York State, August 10

The series returned to Watkins Glen, not for another six-hour endurance test, but for a 250-mile 'sprint' race. Baldi was back driving with Theys, and the Ferrari started from pole.

Always close to the front of the field, Baldi and Theys lost out to the Weaver/Leitzinger Riley & Scott Mk III Ford, finishing second, one lap down on the winning car, due to an unscheduled pit stop to replace the nosecone after running into the back of a GT class Porsche.

Their successful finish concluded a run of six consecutive events where the car had not placed lower than third; a remarkable achievement considering the age of the car's design.

Practice times were good enough to see the Doran-Lista entry on the first row of the grid at Road America.
(Courtesy Tom Schultz)

It was a wet practice day at Watkins Glen, but the Doran team did its best to remain dry. (Courtesy Andrew Hartwell)

It was not a good day for #025 at Watkins Glen – the car sustained accident damage and was forced to retire. (Courtesy Andrew Hartwell)

Europe

Barcelona, April 8

The Sports Racing World Cup had become the FIA Sportscar Championship, and new teams and new cars greeted the fans at the first of the eight-race FIA Sportscar Championship events in Barcelona.

Maybe what they were not expecting, though, was for two aging Ferrari 333 SPs to finish 1-2 in the race. Both the winning Ferraris were entered by BMS Scuderia Italia. Christian Pescatori and Marco Zadra drove the winning car, #024, while Angelo Zadra, Enzo Calderari and Lilian Bryner drove the other one. Pescatori built up an impressive lead and was never challenged, while the other Ferrari was comfortably ahead of third-placed Gary Formato/Mauro Baldi in a Riley & Scott-Judd. A third Ferrari had been entered by GLV Racing, but the 333 SP-Judd lasted only one lap before going out with a broken gearbox.

Monza, April 22

The same three Ferraris turned up for the 'home fixture' at Monza, but the anticipated threat from the two BMS Scuderia Italia Ferraris never materialised. After 29 laps, Marco Zadra's car ground to a halt with electrical problems, and the second team car blew an engine, 83 laps into the race.

It was left to the GLV Brums 333 SP-Judd #003 to score a famous, if improbable, victory over the chasing Ascari A410-Judd, winning by seven seconds. With ten laps to go, Lavaggi had battled his way into the lead, despite being delayed by a faltering starter motor that plagued the car all afternoon. Lavaggi's victory would have been received with mixed feelings at Modena.

Spa, May 13

The long and winding Spa-Francorchamps circuit was the venue for the third round of the series, and the BMS Scuderia Italia team scored their second 1-2 of the year, as the more-fancied runners succumbed to the consistent pace and reliability of the venerable Ferraris. Jean-Marc Gounon joined Marco Zadra, and helped him to his second win of the season, while the second team car finished just five seconds behind.

Meanwhile, Lavaggi's Judd-powered 333 SP started out looking like a force to be reckoned with – the Italian was the fastest qualifier, but the car was found to be slightly underweight and sent to the back of the 17-car grid. Co-driver Christian Vann battled his way up to sixth place, but a broken bleed valve lost him his brakes. The team took seven minutes to repair it. Lavaggi finally managed to finish the car in fifth.

Christian Pescatori

Christian Pescatori was born in Italy in 1971. He began his career in Formula 3, then F3000. He later moved to sports car racing and won the SRWC in 2000, and the FIA GT championships, both for the JMB Racing team.

Christian Pescatori. (Author's collection)

The BMS entry, #029, finished second, behind its sister car at Spa. (Courtesy Paul Kooyman)

Brno, July 1

The trip to Brno ended Ferrari's run of victories in the series. Jean-Marc Gounon had claimed pole, with Hiroki Katoh next to him in a Dome S101-Judd, but Katoh was first away, and stayed ahead of the following pack. The Gounon/Zadra Ferrari stayed in touch for most of the race, finishing 15 seconds behind the winning car. The other BMS Scuderia Italia car never had the same pace, and finished seventh, one lap down.

The GLV Brums 333 SP-Judd was the first car to retire, on lap 18, when the starter motor jammed at the first pit stop with Christian Vann aboard.

Magny-Cours, July 29

Pescatori started on the front row of the grid at Magny-Cours, but he immediately became entangled with Neilson's Dome S101-Judd, forcing the Ferrari onto the grass. An early pit stop cleared the debris from the air intakes, and he set off in pursuit of the pack.

Lavaggi started on the sixth row, but, by lap 12, had pushed his way up to second place, with Pescatori just behind him. On lap 46, the GLV Brums car's gearbox gave way just as it was seeing off the Pescatori threat, leaving Pescatori to inherit second place. Behind him, the consistently-reliable second BMS Ferrari driven by Enzo Calderari, finished two laps down, in fifth.

Donington Park, August 26

Donington Park was the venue for the seventh round of the FIA Sportscar Championship. The Zadra/Gounon car, #024, managed to finish in second place, nearly a minute behind the winning Ascari A410-Judd, but for the other two Ferraris it was a frustrating weekend. The second BMS Scuderia Italia car had a rare non-finish, when a wheel came loose and was in imminent danger of falling off, while Lavaggi's Ferrari developed a clutch problem on the first lap, then later lost fourth gear, but it managed to keep going until lap 95 before finally grinding to a halt.

Mondello Park, September 1

It was no surprise that the GLV Brums car was not repaired in time for the next race, one week later at Mondello Park, so it was left to the two BMS Scuderia Italia cars to claim points towards the Championship.

Pescatori was on the front row, the other 333 SP in seventh. Pescatori's afternoon did not go well. On the 12th lap, he spun after tripping over a slower car, losing time that he and Zadra were not able to make up. They finished second, more than a minute behind the Dome S101-Judd.

The other BMS Scuderia Italia car was never in the hunt and finished eighth, four laps down on the leaders, after relying on a wet setup for what turned out to be a rapidly drying track.

Marco Zadra sits in #024 at Donington. He and co-driver Jean-Marc Gounon finished in second place.
(Courtesy Peter Collins)

#024 waits in the pits during a practice session with Marco Zadra at the wheel. (Courtesy Peter Collins)

Jean-Marc Gounon sits in Ferrari #024 at Donington. (Courtesy Peter Collins)

Nürburgring, September 16

The final round of the FIA Sportscar Championship was held at Nürburgring. It took some luck, canny judgement, and a little help from Marco Zadra's father, Angelo, for Marco Zadra to secure the Sportscar Drivers' Championship. The Pescatori/Zadra car had been in a clear second place, and with Zadra's nearest title-rival a distant fifth, it seemed assured. However, on lap 64, the Ferrari began smoking. Eventually, the oil-gushing gearbox became too bad for the car to continue. Instead of retiring, the car sat in the pits, with the drivers waiting to see how the remainder of the race unfolded. Retirements helped their cause, and then, in the final laps, the second BMS Scuderia Italia Ferrari, driven by Angelo Zadra, pitted and tactically retired, pushing the lame Ferrari up one place. Suddenly Marco Zadra's Ferrari was up to fifth in the SR1 class, earning Marco enough points to take the Championship.

After a good start to the season, the GLV Brums Ferrari once again suffered gearbox problems, and only completed seven laps before retiring.

Grand American Road Race Championship

Date	Race venue	No	Chassis	Entrant	Drivers	Result
4.2.01	Daytona 24hr	12	037	Risi	Kelleners R/Brabham D/McNish A/van de Poele E	dnf
		45	024	BMS Italia	Zadre	dna
		47	029	BMS Italia	–	dna
		12T		Risi	–	unused
19.5.01	Watkins Glen	27	025	Lista Doran	Theys D/Baldi M/Lienhard F	1
28.5.01	Lime Rock	27	025	Lista Doran	Theys D/Baldi M	3
10.6.01	Mid-Ohio	27	025	Lista Doran	Theys D/Baldi M	3
8.7.01	Road America	27	025	Lista Doran	Theys D/Lienhard F/Baldi M	1
5.8.01	Trois-Rivieres	27	025	Lista Doran	Bentley R/Theys D	3
10.8.01	Watkins Glen	27	025	Lista Doran	Baldi M/Theys D	2
3.11.01	Daytona	27	025	Lista Doran	Theys D/Lienhard F	dna

Sports Racing World Cup

Date	Race venue	No	Chassis	Entrant	Drivers	Result
8.4.01	Barcelona	1	024	BMS	Pescatori C/Zadra M	1
		2	029	BMS	Zadra A/Calderari E/Bryner L	2
		3	003	GLV Brums	Vann C/Lavaggi G	dnf
		28	031	Tampolli	Giraudi G	dna
22.4.01	Monza	3	003	GLV Brums	Vann C/Lavaggi G	1
		1	024	BMS	Pescatori C/Zadra M	dnf
		2	029	BMS	Bryner L/Calderari E/Zadra A	dnf
		28	031	Tampolli	Giraudi G	dna

Date	Race venue	No	Chassis	Entrant	Drivers	Result
13.5.01	Spa	1	024	BMS	Zadra M/Gounon J	1
		2	029	BMS	Zadra A/Calderari E/Bryner L	2
		3	003	GLV Brums	Vann C/Lavaggi G	5
1.7.2001	Brno	1	024	BMS	Zadra M/Gounon J	2
		2	029	BMS	Zadra A/Calderari E/Bryner L	7
		3	003	GLV Brums	Vann C/Lavaggi G	dnf
		28	031	Tampolli	Giraudi G	dna
29.7.01	Magny-Cours	1	024	BMS	Pescatori C/Zadra M	2
		2	029	BMS	Bryner L/Calderari E/Zadra A	5
		3	003	GLV Brums	Vann C/Lavaggi G	dnf
		27	031	Tampolli	Giraudi G/Parastili R	dna
26.8.01	Donington	1	024	BMS	Zadra M/Gounon J	2
		2	029	BMS	Bryner L/Calderari E/Zadra A	dnf
		3	003	GLV Brums	Vann C/Lavaggi G	dnf
1.9.01	Mondello	1	024	BMS	Pescatori C/Zadra M	2
		2	029	BMS	Bryner L/Calderari E/Zadra A	8
		3	003	GLV Brums	Vann C/Lavaggi G	dna
16.9.01	Nurburgring	1	024	BMS	Pescatori C/Zadra M	11
		2	029	BMS	Bryner L/Calderari E/Zadra A	dnf
		3	003	GLV Brums	Lavaggi G/Berridge R/Pompidou X	dnf
		27	031	Tampolli	Giraudi G	dna

2002-2003 – 'The Last Hurrah'

Daytona International Raceway, Daytona Beach, Florida, February 3

The 2002 Daytona 24-hour race was to be the final competitive outing for the Risi 333 SP #040. While the car managed to qualify in sixth place, its eight-year old design was becoming very outdated, left behind by the newer technology of its rivals. Despite its advanced age, in the early stages of the race, the Risi Ferrari was in contention, even leading at one point. However, after six hours, a gearbox problem put the 333 SP in the pits for a long time.

In the end, the race's duration was just too much for the car – crippled by two gearbox pinion shaft failures caused by incorrect heat treatment, its chances were finally scuppered by an accident on cold tyres as day was

The Risi team entered #040 in the Daytona 24-hour race. It covered 455 laps in 16 hours, before retiring due to accident damage. (Courtesy Keith Bluemel)

breaking. With David Brabham driving, the car slammed into a barrier. The damage was too serious for it to continue. The 333 SP had covered 455 laps in the 16 hours that it ran.

Daytona International Raceway, Daytona Beach, Florida, November 10

The final competitive appearance of the 333 SP in America was back at Daytona for the three-hour race with a car that has been confirmed to be #001, somewhat modified, and entered by 962.com. Nobody could have guessed that the very first car produced and crashed by Mauro Baldi in testing back in 1994 would be the selfsame car to make the final competitive attempt at victory for the marque on American soil.

The Ferrari qualified 13th out of a field of 43. It did not go out with a flourish, however, withdrawing from the race with gearbox failure after covering 17 laps at the hands of van Schoote and Jackson.

Europe, 2003

Lausitzring, May 10

With only 12 entries and eight starters, Lausitzring was hardly much of a spectacle for the people who turned up to watch. The GLV 333 SP-Judd #003 made no impression on its more high-tech opponents, with Pompidou/Lavaggi finishing sixth, ten laps down on the winning Dome S101-Judd.

Monza, June 29

At Monza, the GLV 333 SP-Judd surprised everyone by taking a first row place on the grid. Its luck was not to last. The 15 cars made a clean start, and the 333 SP was gradually sucked back into the pack. On the 32nd lap, the engine expired and the car was retired.

It was to be the final time that the Ferrari 333 SP was seen in competition in Europe.

The 926.com team entered #001, the very first 333 SP, for the 3-hour race at Daytona held in November. (Courtesy Martin Spetz)

After qualifying in 13th place on the grid, #001 retired with gearbox failure after covering 17 laps of the Daytona track. (Courtesy Martin Spetz)

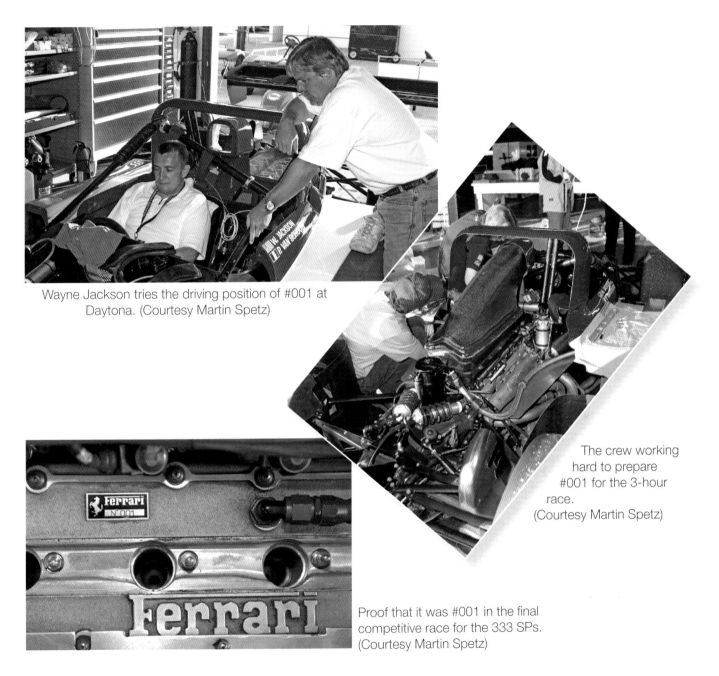

Wayne Jackson tries the driving position of #001 at Daytona. (Courtesy Martin Spetz)

The crew working hard to prepare #001 for the 3-hour race. (Courtesy Martin Spetz)

Proof that it was #001 in the final competitive race for the 333 SPs. (Courtesy Martin Spetz)

#001 is loaded up on the transporter, after failing to finish the Daytona 3-hour race. (Courtesy Martin Spetz)

Grand American Road Race Championship

Date	Race venue	No	Chassis	Entrant	Drivers	Result
3.2.02	Daytona 24hr	13	040	Risi	van de Poele E/Brabham D/Johansson S	36
10.11.02	Daytona	88	001	962.com	van Schoote P/Jackson W	dnf

FIA Sports Racing World Cup

Date	Race venue	No	Chassis	Entrant	Drivers	Result
10.5.03	Lausitzring	3	003	GLV Racing	Pompidou X/Lavaggi G	6
29.6.03	Monza	3	003	GLV Racing	Lavaggi G/Pompidou X	dnf

Visit Veloce on the web – www.veloce.co.uk
Details of all books in print • Special offers • New book news • Gift vouchers • Web forum • And much more ...

Audi

R8

Ian Wagstaff

The history of the world's most successful endurance racing car: the Audi R8. Featuring reports of all of its 80 races, plus profiles of the 35 drivers who raced the car between 2000 and 2006 – as well as the Audi R8R and R8C of 1999. Features individual chassis details, results, and observations from significant individuals involved with the R8.

ISBN: 978-1-845843-27-4
Paperback • 19.5x21cm • £15.99* UK/$29.95* USA • 128 pages • 115 colour and b&w pictures

For more info on Veloce titles, visit our website at www.veloce.co.uk
• email: info@veloce.co.uk • Tel: +44(0)1305 260068
* prices subject to change, p&p extra

The Book of the

Ferrari
288
GTO

Joe Sackey

Foreword by
Ingegnere Nicola Materazzi

Covers the entire story of the iconic Ferrari 288 GTO, including the prototypes, early production cars, mainstream production cars in their various specification guises, and the Evolution cars planned for the aborted Group B FIA race series. A comprehensive and beautifully illustrated look at a unique sports car.

ISBN: 978 1-045842-73-4
Hardback • 25x25cm • £50* UK/$79.95* USA • 272 pages • 326 colour and b&w pictures

For more info on Veloce titles, visit our website at www.veloce.co.uk
• email: info@veloce.co.uk • Tel: +44(0)1305 260068
* prices subject to change, p&p extra

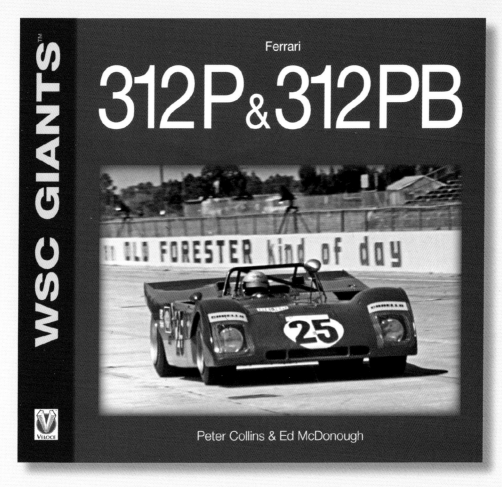

WSC GIANTS

Ferrari

312P & 312PB

Peter Collins & Ed McDonough

Details the origin and history of the 3-litre Ferrari sports cars, which the famed Italian firm designed and built to contest the various versions of the World Sports Car Championship between 1969 and 1973. Features over 100 photographs, many rare and previously unpublished.

ISBN: 978-1-845842-59-8
Paperback • 19.5x21cm • £16.99* UK/$29.95* USA • 128 pages • 145 colour and b&w pictures

For more info on Veloce titles, visit our website at www.veloce.co.uk
• email: info@veloce.co.uk • Tel: +44(0)1305 260068
* prices subject to change, p&p extra

GRAND PRIX

FERRARI

THE YEARS OF ENZO FERRARI'S POWER, 1948-1980

ANTHONY PRITCHARD

A limited edition of 1500 copies. An enthralling, comprehensive, and highly readable account of the racing history of motor sport's most important marque, supported by over 200 colour and black and white photographs.

ISBN: 978-1-845846-23-7
Hardback • 25x25cm • £85* UK/$135* USA • 416 pages • 214 colour and b&w pictures

For more info on Veloce titles, visit our website at www.veloce.co.uk
• email: info@veloce.co.uk • Tel: +44(0)1305 260068
* prices subject to change, p&p extra

Index